THE LONGABERGER
STORY
And How We Did It

Dave Longaberger
with Steve Williford

The Lincoln - Bradley Publishing Group

New York
Memphis *Gatlinburg*

THE LONGABERGER STORY

And How We Did It

The Lincoln-Bradley Publishing Group
P.O. Box 808
Gatlinburg, TN 37738
(615) 436–4762

Manufactured in the United States of America

"Updated, revised and expanded for 1994 and beyond."

Managing Editor: Carl Mays
Cover and Interior Design: Rick Soldin
(Electronic Publishing Services, Inc. – Jonesborough, TN)
Front Cover Photography: Bob Murphy, C.P.P
(Beadling Photography – Zanesville, OH)

Library of Congress Cataloging-in-Publication Data

Williford, Steve
    The Longaberger Story and how we did it/
Steve Williford

    p.   cm.
    ISBN 1-879111-25-X
    1. Success in business.   I. Title

Library of Congress Catalog Number: 90-63930

For the ease of the reader, trademark and service mark notations have been omitted from the text. Among the marks owned by The Longaberger Company are: Longaberger®, Longaberger Baskets®, Longaberger Pottery®, The Bee™, Basket Bee™, Woven Traditions™, Longaberger University®, Longaberger Basket Village™, and Longaberger Farms™.

12 11 10 9 8 7

Dave Longaberger would like to dedicate this book
to his Mother and Dad,
his Brothers and Sisters
and to all the employees, Consultants and customers
who made the dream come true.

PREFACE TO THE ORIGINAL EDITION

When I was first asked to write a book about Dave Longaberger and his baskets, I wasn't too excited. A basket book just didn't sound too thrilling. So, I flew to Dresden, Ohio, lacking enthusiasm.

When I met Dave Longaberger, I knew that I was both wrong and lucky. Wrong about the assignment and lucky to have it.

First of all, in the midst of his good time, he'd developed a $30 million dollar business with over 1,000 employees and 4,000 Sales Consultants (I'll give you an update on those figures in just a minute).

Second, he built a labor intensive business in a time when factories were closing instead of growing and sales were being lost to the foreign markets.

Third, he's had problems. Many and major. He failed in school. Banks wouldn't loan him money to start a business. He's been over a million dollars in debt. His factory burned with practically no insurance. He was faced with a major, emotional lawsuit. He was faced with a union effort. But he survived each of these crises and learned from them.

Fourth, Dave is a people person from the word go. People trust him and they like him. I like him too.

I went to his plants and observed the basket making process. I was immediately taken by the craftsmanship of the baskets. I was amazed that the process began with actual trees in the Hartville plant and ended with baskets in the Dresden plants.

I was impressed by the pride of workmanship and the productivity of the employees.

I was impressed by the creative structure of basket sales and the energy, enthusiasm, personality and warmth of the Sales Consultants. They love Longaberger Baskets.

I realized that whatever Dave Longaberger was doing, I wanted to find out more. Because he was doing something that the rest of us needed to know.

Steve Williford — 1988

PREFACE TO THE SIXTH EDITION

Welcome to the sixth edition of *The Longaberger Story and How We Did It.* The exciting aspect of this story to me, other than the fact that I've been fortunate enough to continue following it, is that the story grows and picks up momentum.

For example, in the last six years since the original book was published, Dave Longaberger has built over 1,000,000 square feet of plant space for his employees. Speaking of employees, the count has quadrupled. As you might also imagine, the Longaberger Sales Consultants have grown over the past years. It's been a controlled growth, to prevent demand from exceeding production capabilities, but the growth has still been significant – over 20,000.

Sales have also increased – dramatically. From $30 million to over $200 million a year.

The little town of Dresden, Ohio has undergone a major face lift. Longaberger spearheaded a move to not only paint up and fix up, but to put in new sidewalks, grass, trees and baskets up and down Main Street. And then there's the incredible back to the '50s Popeye's Soda Fountain, the Longaberger Museum (that's right, a real museum, complete with a theater and a live weaver at work), the Longaberger Restaurant, the Village Etc. shop, the World's Largest Basket Park, the charming Main Street shops, the Kenny Wolford Community Park that you have to see to believe, the Swimming Center which includes an olympic sized outdoor swimming complex and restaurant/pavilion facility, the Senior Citizens Center, Jayhawks Dairy Bar, the Station House Meeting and Banquet Facility, and the Renovated Train Depot. Longaberger also more than doubled the size of the existing high school, Tri-Valley High, paying for 23 classrooms and a vocational-agricultural building. Longaberger has also helped several other nearby schools expand their facilities. These are some of the reasons why Longaberger received the *Vision for Tomorrow Award* from the Direct Selling Association, the *Take Pride in America Award* from the U.S. Department of the Interior and the *Socially Responsible Entrepreneur of the Year Award* from *Inc.* Magazine.

Another major development over the past few years has been **Longaberger Pottery.** Longaberger Manufacturing has included Longaberger Pottery in a big way. The pottery is custom designed and crafted with the same skill and sense of history as the baskets.

Exciting growth is taking place throughout The Longaberger Company. The sales field continues to post new records under Tami Longaberger's leadership. Meanwhile, manufacturing, under Rachel Longaberger Schmidt's guidance and through innovative team concepts and benefits, is able to fulfill the constantly growing product demand.

The *Longaberger Story* grows more exciting every year. Hang on to this book because it will soon be a collector's item. Even with the many changes and accomplishments of the past few years, things will continue to progress and grow. I have a feeling that five years from this edition, readers will smile, shake their heads and be barely able to believe that Longaberger was as small as it is today.

The good news is that it's still a great time to become a Consultant. Annual sales reach less than 10% of the United States.

Steve Williford — 1994

CONTENTS

LONGABERGER STORY BACKGROUND

It took Dave Longaberger a while to complete his high school education. That's because he spent two years in the first grade and three in the fifth. He also suffered severely from stuttering and epilepsy, and he grew up in a family of 14 with one bathroom.

But Dave Longaberger had a philosophy. He felt that successful business was very simple. "Business is so easy it's pathetic," he was often heard to say. He felt that he could be successful in tiny Dresden, Ohio . . . selling baskets.

Most of his friends and acquaintances told him to drop his idea. First, the basket industry was controlled by foreign manufacturers. Second, he'd built a successful grocery store and restaurant business and to do what he wanted with his "basket dream" would require staking his present success on his future idea. Third, factories across the nation were closing, not opening.

So he began. He asked a few ladies if they would consider making baskets for him. He had the old molds from his father. He knew the baskets lasted from one generation to the next. He felt that the baskets that were made for farmers also had marketability to homeowners. Only one problem – he was unable to pay the ladies for the first two months. They went to work anyway.

Out of that humble beginning, The Longaberger Company is still selling baskets. As a matter of fact, it's selling millions of baskets. The questions are many:

How did a man who barely graduated from high school, actually, who *barely graduated from elementary school,* achieve such success?

How did Dave Longaberger start a thriving manufacturing business when thousands of factories were closing?

Why are Longaberger Baskets so popular?

How did Longaberger get from a few dozen baskets to a few million baskets in sales?

Why did Dave quit selling his baskets in stores?

How did that lead to such a dramatic sales increase?

But beyond these questions, what can *you* learn from Dave Longaberger and The Longaberger Company? Are his visionary methods and principles adaptable to your goals and dreams?

Yes. Dave Longaberger was labeled a failure. But he had talents. They simply went unrecognized. He chose not to believe what others said about who he was and what he could do. There's a message there for a lot of us. The Longaberger Company began with no start up money. It was designed to sell a quality product at a fair price. It was also designed to share profits with those who sold the products. It's a very simple marketing idea that has worked well.

J.W. LONGABERGER, DAVE'S FATHER, FORMING THE BOTTOM OF A WARE BASKET IN 1953.

THE PAST

FLOSSIE, THE COW THAT WASN'T...

Dave Longaberger probably still holds the record at the Dresden Grade School for most years spent there – nine.

He spent two years in the first grade and three in the fifth. He also suffered from severe stuttering and epilepsy. Little did anyone realize that one day, Dave Longaberger would be the town's major employer, the largest handmade basket manufacturer in the world . . . and Chairman of the Board and Chief Executive Officer of one of the top direct sales companies in the world.

For example, Dave's early education began to devastate his self-esteem. Mrs. Skelly, Dave's first grade teacher, would ask Dave to stand up to read "and the class would start laughing at me," Dave recalled, "because of my stuttering and I'd sit down.

"My confidence began building in the fourth grade when Mrs. Gibson made me remain standing even when others would laugh at my stuttering. 'No Popeye,' she'd say when I sat down, 'you just stay up there and read.' I did and they finally quit laughing."

School was not for Dave. "He had other fish to fry," Bonnie Longaberger, his mother, remembered. Dave would sit and stare out the window. "That great big world out there," Dave recalled, "for me to run in, and she (his fifth grade teacher) was keeping me from it. I thought, 'I'll show her,' but after repeating the fifth grade so many times, I decided that she was winning!

"Actually, I thought my fifth grade teacher, Ruby Adams, was in love with me because she kept me in her class so many years."

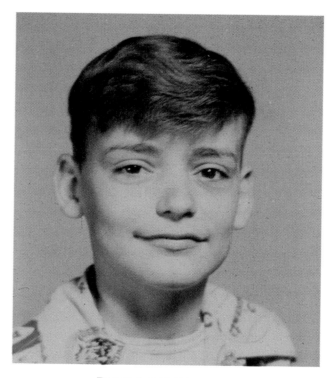

DAVE LONGABERGER

When Dave was seven years old, he began his employment history at Fred Shoemaker's neighborhood grocery store. From then on, every time the store was sold, Dave was counted as part of the store's inventory. Before most children ever thought about work, Dave or "Popeye," as his friends began to call him, had been employed by several different owners, each with different personalities and business philosophies.

Although his education inside the Dresden Grade School wasn't helping much, Dave's real classroom became the corner grocery. For example, he learned the easiest way to keep the boss off his back was to do the work before he was told. So Dave dusted and straightened the shelves, swept the sidewalk and then went to school. He returned to the grocery to stock the shelves and do other work that was needed. Eventually, he was able to create displays and organize the food as he thought best.

Dave observed the bad with the good. He saw poor people skills and good ones. He saw quality prioritized, but also observed dishonesty emphasized. For example, during World War II, he witnessed some black marketing of meat and was told, "Popeye, go in the back and weigh five pounds of sugar and flour but only put four and a half pounds in the sack." Or, "Popeye, go back and grind hamburger with crackers (to make it weigh more)." "I saw them weigh their fingers on the scales more than once too."

> HE LEARNED THE EASIEST WAY TO KEEP THE BOSS OFF HIS BACK WAS TO DO THE WORK BEFORE HE WAS TOLD.

Dave learned about his own ethics during this period. Take for example the time he decided to go swimming instead of working at the grocery. It was a hot summer day and all of his friends were at the swimming hole. Dave slipped out of the store while the owner, Mr. Frank McClintock, wasn't looking.

J.W.

Of course he hightailed it down to the pond, swam for a bit and ran back to the store. When Frank asked where he'd been, Dave said, "Oh, I was in the back with the stock." Frank directed Dave to a mirror to see his hair sticking up in every direction.

"I learned that it doesn't pay to lie," Dave said.

There was another time when he relearned the lesson. Dave was taking an agriculture class in school ("I took the class because of the field trips"). A prerequisite for the class was to have a farm project. Dave's project was a calf. There was only one problem. Dave didn't have a calf.

> "I KNEW AND HE KNEW AND WE KNEW EACH OTHER KNEW," DAVE LAUGHED. "THAT WAS A PAINFUL LESSON, BUT I TOLD MYSELF IF I EVER GOT OUT OF THAT BUS ALIVE, I'D NEVER TELL ANOTHER LIE. WELL, I'VE TOLD A FEW MORE SINCE THEN, BUT THAT'S ALWAYS STUCK WITH ME. THE EASIEST WAY OUT OF ANY SITUATION IS TO TELL THE TRUTH."

As the year progressed, the dishonesty escalated. For example, Dave had to report on his calf's status, including: what time he fed it, how much it weighed and even what time it went to bed.

Then one day it happened. The teacher, Mr. Robert "Mac" McMurray, announced, "Class, today we're going to take a trip to see your calves first-hand." Dave's heart almost stopped. He got on the bus and sat in the back and felt his heart beat faster and faster with every stop they made.

The teacher finally said, "And now, let's go see Dave's calf, Flossie." Dave sat wide-eyed as the bus neared Flossie's theoretical location. At a fork in the road, the teacher said, "No, I've changed my mind. Let's go see Dave Graves' calf instead. Sorry Dave. I don't think we'll have time to see Flossie."

"I knew and he knew and we knew each other knew," Dave laughed. "That was a painful lesson, but I told myself if I ever got out of that bus alive, I'd never tell another lie. Well, I've told a few more since then, but that's always stuck with me. The easiest way out of any situation is to tell the truth."

The Twenty-Five Cent Millionaire

In addition to the grocery business, Dave also found work shoveling snow, mowing grass, delivering papers and hauling trash. His family began calling him "the 25 cent millionaire."

Dave's sister, Ginny Lou Wilcox, remembered a Mother's Day when ten year old Dave bought his mother a wooden chest full of candy. They found out later that he bought it on credit, something unheard of at this store. Dave negotiated a payment plan with the owner of Messenger's Dime Store for a dollar a week.

"He could do things like that," Ginny said. "Dave could talk a person into lending on credit when no other person in this town could."

"That's because everyone in town knew that he would pay them back, even at age ten," Wendy Little, another sister added.

But they didn't just lend, they bought too! Take, for example, the story of the little red radio.

The Little Red Radio

Dave's school sponsored a magazine contest when he was in the seventh grade. The grand prize was a little red radio. Dave recalled, "I took one look at that little red radio and I knew it was mine."

"I knew I could use it because we camped out and we could take it with us."

But *how?* How could Dave Longaberger compete with the other kids in school? This was a kid who had been in school for ten years and was only in the seventh grade. One younger brother had passed him in school and a younger sister was in his same grade. Besides that, he stuttered terribly, particularly when nervous.

Dave marched out in the neighborhood, began his sales pitch and would begin stuttering. "They would say, 'Oh Popeye, just give me the book and show me where to sign,'" Dave remembered. So he began making some sales and proudly turned his money in only to discover that Marilyn Evans, the best looking and most likely to succeed girl in the seventh grade, turned in more. Each day he turned in money, she turned in more.

He decided that if he was to win the little red radio, he was going to have to create a new strategy. His new strategy became a process he would use throughout his life. He called it, *Look, Think, Do.*

First, he looked at the situation. The problem was that every time he turned in his money, Marilyn would turn in more. Then he thought about it. "The principal said he *wanted* us to turn in our money every day, but he didn't say we *had* to. If I don't turn in all of my money every day, maybe Marilyn will think she's so far ahead she'll quit trying so hard."

On the final day, Dave turned in $350.00 and won by over $200.00. Although the principal was not amused, Dave won the little red radio. He also learned that if you want something so much you can taste it, you'll often find a way.

THE BIRTH OF THE BASKETS

Dave Longaberger was one of 12 children. But before we talk about this era, let's take a step further back in time.

The year was 1896 when John and Carrie Longaberger moved to Dresden, Ohio, a small farming community of a few hundred people, hidden in the rolling forested hills of central Ohio.

John found work at the Dresden Basket Factory which made several different types of baskets by hand for a variety of practical uses. Baskets were utilized for functions that today are associated with cardboard boxes or plastic.

DADDY JOHN LONGABERGER

John and Carrie had a son, John Wendell, "J.W," in 1902. Throughout his childhood, J.W. learned to love the baskets, first helping clean up around the shop and then making basket bottoms. J.W. finally left high school at 17 to join his father as a full-time basket maker to help support the family. He quickly became an excellent craftsman, reflecting his love for the trade.

**J.W.
LONGABERGER**

**BONNIE
LONGABERGER**

**DOWNTOWN DRESDEN
MAINSTREET IN EARLY 1930'S**

He took great pride in seeing his baskets loaded with a farmer's produce for the market or used by the ladies to transport groceries home from the market.

J.W. married Bonnie Jean Gist in 1927 and rented a house on the same property as the Dresden Basket Factory.

But when the Great Depression hit, the basket industry fell on hard times, forcing the factory's owner to sell. J.W. bought it and the house for $1900.00. He changed the name to the Ohio Ware Basket Company.

Meanwhile, the Longaberger family was growing. With six children, J.W. found that making baskets wasn't enough income. So he worked at the Dresden Paper Mill during the day and made baskets at night. He sold each basket for about $1.50.

In addition to making the baskets, he found the best trees in the woods, cut them down, hauled them 80 miles away to Marietta to be made into splints, went back and collected the splints, brought them back to Dresden, laid them out in the yard to dry and then placed them in racks in the workshop.

**THE OLD OHIO WARE BASKET SHOP,
WHEN J.W. & BONNIE BOUGHT IT IN 1936.**

J.W. created shapes and sizes of baskets in response to the local needs. For example, when the pottery factories were booming, he created large pottery baskets. When the pottery business slowed down, he created special baskets such as fruit baskets (with inverted bottoms for farmers which allowed air to circulate and prevent rotting), market baskets, corn baskets and laundry baskets.

Bonnie began to work at the Dresden Woolen Mill, in between six more children. Dave was born the fifth of six boys with six sisters. All but one (the last) were born at home.

> **DAVE WOULD LATER SAY HIS GOAL IN LIFE WAS TO HAVE HIS OWN BATHROOM.**

Their home had three bedrooms, a living room, a dining room, kitchen and one bathroom!

"We kids didn't realize we were poor," sister Ginny Lou Wilcox said. "We didn't have bicycles; we didn't have roller skates; we didn't have a lot of things that kids take for granted, but we didn't know and we didn't care."

FIVE OF THE 12
LONGABERGER
CHILDREN. DAVE IS
IN J.W.'S ARMS.

NINE OF THE 12 CHILDREN.
DAVE IS THE SECOND ON LEFT, FRONT ROW.

"We always had something for dessert," according to sister, Judy Swope. "It was usually rice or bread pudding, which is why Dave still hates bread puddings."

"I'm very proud of my family," Dave reflected. "I think all of the 12 kids became successes in their own right."

As cardboard and paper sacks began to replace the uses of baskets, J.W.'s business declined. But he still continued to make baskets in his spare time.

LEARN FROM THE PAST!

In those early years, Dave learned many valuable philosophies that he continues to use today. As a matter of fact, if you listen to him very long, you'll hear him say that it's very difficult to separate the present from the past and future. After all, the present is the sum total of the past, and the future is built on the present. "Learn from the past," Dave insists. "Use the lessons you learned to make today more successful."

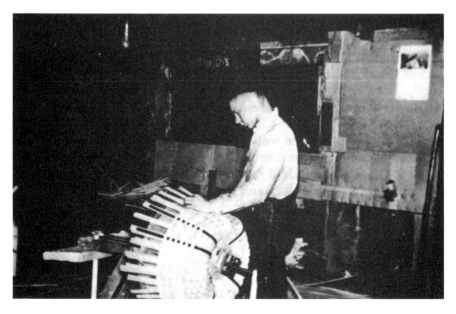

LARRY LONGABERGER, DAVE'S BROTHER,
MAKING A POTTERY BASKET IN THE '50S.

**THE SWIMMING HOLE, 1953.
PHOTOGRAPHER: DAVE.**

For example, a frequent Longaberger philosophy comes from what Dave calls "your insurance policy." The kids in Dresden loved to swim in the creek. The rule was, however, to stay out of the water unless there was someone there capable of lifesaving.

"If you were caught in the water without someone on the bank, the older kids would really give it to you," Dave said. "I've used that rule thousands of times in my life. I never go into a new business venture unless there's someone on the bank to save me. If there's no one to save me, I stay very close to the bank!"

THERE'S NO WEAKNESS IN FORGIVENESS

The rule at the Longaberger home was *be in at 12, six and nine o'clock or else.* "Dad had a great incentive program," Dave smiled. "It was called the belt."

Ten-year old Dave was playing basketball one evening for "the NBA Championship" when he noticed it was darker than usual.

"What time is it?" he asked, holding his breath.

"Seven o'clock."

Fear went through him like a surge of electricity. He bolted for home, through the school playground where his sisters and brothers were playing, after having already eaten dinner at six.

"They loved it because they knew I was about to get killed."

The closer he got, the more he panicked. On the one hand, he thought, "He surely won't whip me because I forgot what time it is."

On the other hand, he thought, "He's not going to whip me because I'm not going home!" So he started down the railroad track and in less than half an hour, had planned his future. He would go to Zanesville, 16 miles away, and spend the next few years shoveling snow and mowing grass until he could go to Chicago . . . or New York . . . or Los Angeles.

> **"DAD HAD A GREAT INCENTIVE PROGRAM," DAVE SMILED. "IT WAS CALLED THE BELT."**

Meanwhile, it was pitch black and he was standing in the middle of the railroad tracks. That's when he decided, "Well, maybe I'll go home, get my whipping, go to bed and it'll all be over in a few minutes."

So he crept up to the house and peeked in the window. His father was sitting in his easy chair, listening to the radio. Feeling that discretion was the better part of valor, Dave opted for the kitchen door. His mother put her fingers to her mouth for Dave to keep quiet, "but she didn't have to do that. I *knew* to keep quiet!"

He said, "I'm going upstairs and go to bed."

"No, you're going to eat," she said as she pulled out his chair. Then she walked over to the oven to a plate she left prepared for him. She took off the cover and Dave ate as fast as he could, partly from hunger and mostly from sheer terror.

All of a sudden, he heard footsteps, looked up and there was his father in the doorway. That's when Dave burst into tears. "I hit a gusher," Dave remembered. "I was crying and sobbing uncontrollably." His father, J.W., looked down at him and said, "Popeye, don't you ever do that again," and walked back to his easy chair.

"That episode is one of the greatest memories that I have of my father," Dave said. "He taught me a valuable lesson that I carry with me every day of my life. You must always give people a second or third chance. My father gave me a second chance and I will never ever forget that. We try to run our business with that lesson in mind. If I had to sum up what I've learned from my mother and father that I use in business today, it's be strong, be firm, but be fair."

> "MY FATHER GAVE ME A SECOND CHANCE AND I WILL NEVER EVER FORGET THAT. IF I HAD TO SUM UP WHAT I'VE LEARNED FROM MY MOTHER AND FATHER THAT I USE IN BUSINESS TODAY, IT'S BE STRONG, BE FIRM, BUT BE FAIR."

THE DRESDEN VARSITY BASKETBALL TEAM.
THE JEFFERSON JAY-HAWKS' #18 IS RICHIE LONGABERGER,
#20 IS DAVE.

LOOK BACK AND GO AHEAD

Dave Longaberger believes in the power of the past. He uses experiences that others might call trivial to provide a basis for what many would call major decisions.

"Everything we do, like it or not, is directly related to our past. Your future is built on your past. 'But I don't like my past,' you say. I say there's some good in your past. The past can help motivate you.

"The past is a foundation. Without it, you can't build. I suggest that you go away for a day or two and think about your past – good times and bad – where you went wrong – and perhaps what you need to do differently next time."

> **"I SUGGEST THAT YOU GO AWAY FOR A DAY OR TWO AND THINK ABOUT YOUR PAST — GOOD TIMES AND BAD — WHERE YOU WENT WRONG — AND PERHAPS WHAT YOU NEED TO DO DIFFERENTLY NEXT TIME."**

Dave's work experiences began at the grocery store and extended in his teenage years to running the projectors at the local theater.

"First, there was Fred Shoemaker's grocery. Then he sold out to Frank McClintock. Frank sold to Earl Starner and he finally sold to Flossie and Russell Messenger. In each case I went along with the stock."

"It seemed to me that Flossie and Russell argued and bickered most of the time. I wasn't used to that so I asked Tom Coins, the owner of the local 135 seat theater, if I could help with the movies. I was about 16 or 17."

One of Dave's most eventful nights at the theater occurred the time he heard that his teacher, DeWitt Ring, would be attending the evening's feature. "For some reason, that really made me nervous," Dave remembered. "I was always impressed with DeWitt Ring. I wanted to do the best job possible."

So Dave arrived at the theater two hours early to preview each reel of the movie for tape breaks and carbon outages. Satisfied that he was fully

THE DRESDEN MOVIE HOUSE

prepared, Dave began the first reel on projector one and adeptly cued projector two at exactly the precise time to allow not the slightest tape lag.

However, in his fervor to preview, Dave inadvertently cued the cartoon reel instead of the next reel of the movie. As Dave described the scene, "John Wayne was about to catch the bandits but caught Woody Woodpecker instead. Mr. Ring kidded me about that for months!

> JOHN WAYNE WAS ABOUT TO CATCH THE BANDITS BUT CAUGHT WOODY WOODPECKER INSTEAD.

"Whenever I worked, I tried to think of the customers as *my* customers and the workplace as mine. I was always looking for a way to improve it."

"I learned a lot through sports too. John Hadden, my basketball coach, said, 'Dave if you ever want to play basketball for us, learn good defense. The best way to do it, look them in the eye.' I think it's the same in business. I call it LTE, Look them in the eye."

A Young Dream

Dave loved to dream. He did it in the classroom. He did it while playing games on Machine Gun Hill.

"We called it that because we helped end the war by shooting so many of the enemy. After the war, we went back to playing Cowboys and Indians."

Dave especially loved to dream at night under an open sky. He and his friends camped on Machine Gun Hill several nights a week during the summer. It gave them a chance to talk about dreams and ideas. "It also gave us the chance to sneak some warm beer up there," Dave smiled. "A beer truck had wrecked in town and beer was everywhere. We wondered what it would be like to get drunk and found out. It was years before I tasted beer again and still don't like it to this day."

"I learned the price for picking up something that didn't belong to me. But on our campouts, we did have a chance to dream about what was to come."

It was like the center of the universe to them. Under a sky exploding with stars. On top of a hill where they could see the lights of tiny Dresden below. The crackle of the campfire. Adolescent conversation and giggles. "But it also gave me a time to think about who I was," Dave said. "What I would like to do, where I'd like to go and what my life was going to be about."

WHAT HAPPENS AFTER HIGH SCHOOL TO A KID WHO SPENT THREE EXTRA YEARS THERE?

That's what Dave Longaberger was asking himself. College didn't seem like a sane choice. His job history consisted of very small grocery stores and a theater. As Dave remembers:

"Finally I graduated from high school! I was very insecure. I wasn't taking myself too seriously. My self-esteem was very low. Because what could I do? I was only reading at a fifth or sixth grade level. How was a dumb kid like myself going to go anywhere in life?"

I think it's interesting that although this sounds like the plot of a novel, Dave didn't know the rest of the story yet! This was happening to Dave Longaberger for the first time. Not only did he not know that he would one day be CEO and Chairman of the Board of a multi-million dollar company, he didn't know what he'd be doing *next week.* If anything, he was getting the other type of signals. Signals such as would he amount to anything? What type of a job could he hope to secure? And he recognized that whatever job he was able to land, he'd begin at the bottom, probably never to move up from that position.

Dave's first job caused a lot of people to laugh. He began selling Fuller Brushes door to door. It's been said that you should do the thing you fear most. If you can do that, chances are you can do anything. Well, what could be harder for a stutterer whose self-confidence was shaky? Dave used his "Look, Think, Do" philosophy.

> **ALTHOUGH THIS SOUNDS LIKE THE PLOT OF A NOVEL, DAVE DIDN'T KNOW THE REST OF THE STORY YET!**

Look: "Who will hire me? I'm not exactly over qualified. I don't see too many options for employment."

Think: "My only chance is to hire myself. I'll be in control and can determine my advancement. I'll have no one to blame if I don't do well. I need more self-confidence. This will help. I seem to relate well to people. They like me. I can make them laugh. This won't be something

I'll do the rest of my life, but it can help me gain skills while I'm deciding."

Do: "Where do I start?"

Dave's little red radio had aged several years since the last time he'd sold door to door. So, off he went to see if his technique would work again. Not the stuttering gimmick. Just Dave. Dave being himself, asking if they needed a brush. But Dave's approach was more involved than just asking for the sale. "The more I sold, the less I stuttered. I think the opportunity to speak should be stressed in elementary school as well as in high school. I thought of these people as *my* customers, not Fuller Brush's. I worked very hard to guarantee customer satisfaction and I found that they liked that. I got so excited. I learned that customer satisfaction had nothing to do with intelligence!"

> **"I LEARNED THAT CUSTOMER SATISFACTION HAD NOTHING TO DO WITH INTELLIGENCE!"**

He created a system. He sold on Mondays, Tuesdays, Wednesdays and Thursdays. He mailed the orders on Fridays and would make deliveries on the weekend for orders taken the previous week. The only trouble was the customers didn't have to pay until they received the brushes and they would sometimes hide from him. "I ended up reselling half of my merchandise," he laughed.

Dave saw the problem of collecting the money a few days after the sale. That's why years later he would collect basket and pottery sales money on the front-end. This allowed the company to pay the weavers and Consultants and continue to grow, a technique directly attributable to Dave's Fuller Brush days.

Dave also organized some of his sisters to sell the brushes, but as Ginny Lou admitted later, "I would ask if they wanted anything and when they said no, we'd drink a cup of coffee and I'd go home."

SERVING TIME

After a few months of selling door to door, Dave heard of an opening at Kaiser Aluminum in Newark, Ohio, at $150 a week. Thinking that he had finally arrived, Dave folded his Fuller suitcase and began working in the Kaiser book mold department between two very hot furnaces. He worked 30 minutes and rested 30. He knew this was not for him.

"I would get off at three o'clock and all I could think about was not wanting to go back. I called it jail. I did not enjoy it."

"Don't get me wrong. I have respect for anyone who works in a factory, including Kaiser. Many of them really enjoyed it. I didn't. Little did I realize that those two disappointing weeks were to be experience enough to start my own factory 20 years later. I saw enough of what I didn't like to structure it the way I *would* have enjoyed it."

PEOPLE SKILLS: THE COMMON DENOMINATOR

Then Dave found out that Cannon's Bakery needed a route man, selling bread, rolls and buns to stores and restaurants. Dave thought, "This is it. I've worked in small grocery stores and I get along well with people."

Art Cannon gave Dave the route. Dave began to learn the business and discovered many similarities between it and every other job he'd had: people skills.

Interestingly enough, Dave went from $150 at Kaiser's to about $75 per week at Cannon's. "I had an opportunity to learn for the future," Dave explained. "And I enjoyed it. Money doesn't make you happy.

"I'll tell you this. There is not a single college or university in the world that could have taught me the knowledge I learned at Cannon's Bakery during those four years."

Dave learned that work could be fun. "I saw the more fun the customers had, the more they bought and continued to buy. I learned the more I enjoyed the work, the more the customers did.

"I found my true world. It was selling. From the magazines, to groceries, to brushes, to bread, to restaurants, to baskets, to a town restoration, to other franchising projects, to myself. And I believe no matter who you are, you have to continue to sell."

After four years, Dave moved from Cannon's Bakery with four trucks to Nickles Bakery with 400 trucks. It was quite an adjustment and again the question was: "Can I do it?"

The supervisor showed him the route, the customers and the stores. As they were driving by two particular stores, the supervisor said, "Don't even waste your time going in those two stores. We've tried and couldn't, so there's no use of *you* trying."

Well, to Dave, the gauntlet had been thrown down! This was a challenge. "I knew they were going to be mine, just like I knew the little red radio was going to be mine," he said.

Isn't it interesting to watch Dave Longaberger's confidence level steadily increase? It also seemed to correspond to what he enjoyed doing. Although he still wasn't on his final career path, his momentum seemed to be increasing. But then, *any* momentum would have been an improvement over his school years.

After a couple of weeks on the route for Nickles, Dave stopped at the two stores in question and asked if they'd like to buy any of his products. "No," the owner replied. "You people have tried to get in here before and we already have plenty of bread companies who supply us."

"Thank you," Dave said and left.

Dave knew he was going to get those stores as customers, but *how?*

He kept thinking about it each day. As he was driving by the stores one day, he noticed a couple of ladies in the parking lot. He drove up, introduced himself and said, "Ladies, I will give you each a cake if you will do me a favor. I would like for you to go in this store and this other store and ask for Nickles' pastries and bread." They did!

So, a couple of days later, sales representative Longaberger casually walked into the stores and asked, "Would you be interested in Nickles products for your store?"

"Yes," the owner said, "As a matter of fact a lady was in here just the other day and asked for Nickles bread."

Dave got space in both stores and one of the stores turned out to be his best account.

"I was so proud to be working for Nickles," Dave said. "They are a great company and take pride in their trucks, their products and their people. I had never seen anything like that in my life. They were the best. I learned the importance and power of pride in what you do."

COMPETITION

Dave carried those lessons with him. He also learned a great deal about competition.

This was the first time that he was faced with several business competitors. It was also the first time that he was aggressively and consistently victimized by the competition. "They would take pens and shoot ink in the packages. They would poke holes in the wrapper, causing the bread to get stale. They would mash our products. Or they would cover ours up with theirs."

The question was how to fight them without getting into a bread throwing contest? As Dave recalls, "I was not a fighter and I certainly well didn't want to love them!"

His solution was simple, strategic and effective. He befriended them.

"Within six months, half of the competition weren't damaging my bread. The other half, well there's not too much reasoning you can do with them. We began to look out for each other, which was strange since we were competitors, but it worked. If I saw Wonder Bread was covered up, I would uncover it. If he saw Nickles covered up, he would uncover our products. I found out there are all sorts of ways to win.

"And just as important to the process, I was learning to see what people wanted. Not what I wanted or the company wanted, but what the *customer* wanted. Through my bread route, I saw that the stores and restaurants who built their businesses around their customers, not themselves, won. And it was the business with the *better* product, not always the cheaper one, that excelled. Those were the places that were full!"

> **"I FOUND OUT THERE ARE ALL SORTS OF WAYS TO WIN. I WAS LEARNING TO SEE NOT WHAT I WANTED OR THE COMPANY WANTED, BUT WHAT THE CUSTOMER WANTED."**

ONE FOR THE MONEY, TWO FOR THE SHOW, THREE TO GET READY AND...ABOUT THAT MONEY

Dave was then selected by Uncle Sam to join the Army. It was there that he understood the advantages of uniformity and control. "I think business should exemplify the military to that degree. You need consistency and you need a central headquarters with clear controls in place," Dave said.

Dave enjoyed the Army through his humor. "Through the humor, I could take the negative while absorbing the positive." Take for example the time he and a few of his buddies concocted a device which included a hot water bottle and tubing. When the bottle was squeezed, whatever it contained was emitted through the tubing.

One night Dave and his Army friends entered a bar. One of the friends was wearing the hot water bottle inside his shirt. The contents contained vegetable soup . . . After a few drinks, the soldier said, "I think I'm going to be sick," and gave the bottle a squeeze.

Dave and his friends rushed to their friend, to apparently assist him. Instead, however, they scrutinized what they knew was vegetable soup, picked up a pea or carrot off the floor and began munching. Humor in uniform.

Dave remembered, "We cleaned the whole bar out when we did it. Our sides hurt for a week."

After serving in the Army, Dave returned to Dresden. By this time a few things had changed. He was older, 29. He was married to Laura Eschman and had a daughter, Tami, born in 1961.

Dave was back on his bread route. They were living in an old house on Chestnut Street that Laura's parents had given them.

Word spread that Harry's Dairy Bar was up for sale. It was a tiny restaurant consisting of eight stools, two booths, two tables and a parking lot. "It was the place in town where everyone went to congregate," Dave reflected. Harry and Marge Lowe were known for their thick milk shakes and the largest ham sandwiches in the state.

HARRY'S DAIRY BAR, SOON TO BECOME POPEYE'S DAIRY BAR.

When Dave heard about it, he got that little red radio feeling all over again. "I knew as soon as I heard that Harry wanted to sell, the dairy bar was to be mine."

But as is often the case for Dave's goals, how? He applied his LTD system to it. Just through observation (Look), it was the most popular place in town, with a reputation for good food and service. Dave thought (Think), "I have over eight years of experience on a bread route, in and out of restaurants and stores. I know from that if you give good service and provide quality food, people will be there to buy. I can do that."

But first he had to buy the restaurant (Do). The price was $15,000, which Dave thought was fair. The only problem was that he didn't have it. So he went down to the bank to get a loan and experienced one of the worst disappointments of his life.

Dave assumed that he could go to the bank, use his house and the restaurant for collateral and begin his new career. He was about to learn that not everyone is in a service business. Unfortunately, many banks weren't then and still aren't today.

After Dave explained what he wanted to do, he added the two collateral pieces together: their home – $6,000, and the dairy bar – $10,000, or $16,000 collateral for a $15,000 loan.

> **THE PRICE WAS $15,000, WHICH DAVE THOUGH WAS FAIR. THE ONLY PROBLEM WAS THAT HE DIDN'T HAVE IT.**

The banker then asked, "What do you know about the restaurant business?"

Dave told him of his experience on the bread routes and grocery stores and how he knew the people in the town and they knew him. "I know from my past experience I can do it," he concluded. The banker knew that. He'd known Dave for years.

The banker thought it was a bad risk and would count the collateral as only $7,000.

"I thought I was going to die," Dave said. "I was disappointed. As I look back, that banker did me a big favor. Don't depend on banks. Only depend on people who believe in you. People think the first thing you need to start a business is money. Well, that's not always true."

Dave approached Harry and Marge with the bad news. Harry said, "Dave, why don't you come back tomorrow? We need to think about this."

Of course, Dave was there bright and early to hear what Harry had to say. "Dave, we can't think of any two people we would want to have our restaurant more than Popeye and Laura. So, we'll take what you can get from the bank and a second mortgage for the rest."

"Harry and Marge, I love you!" Dave said as he started his dash to the bank. "I think I only hit the sidewalk once," Dave laughed.

Out of breath, Dave told the good news to the banker.

"We will have to have a co-signer," the banker replied.

If Dave didn't realize it before, the truth became apparent. "This man didn't want me to have the restaurant."

Instead of encouraging new enterprise and entering into a supportive posture, the bank did exactly the opposite.

Dave was despondent. "I died again." Just when he thought he had overcome every obstacle, another was placed in his way. This proved to be an excellent training ground for later seemingly insurmountable crises.

He didn't know who to ask to co-sign. He would not ask his family. Who else was there? He began to reconsider the supervisor's job Nickles Bakery was offering, when he was telling his friend, Kenny Martin, his story.

Kenny owned Martin's Dairy and was one of the bank's largest customers. Before Dave could finish his feelings about the episode, Kenny took him by the arm and charged into the bank.

They walked into the banker's office and paused. Kenny looked at the banker for several seconds, then broke the silence, "Where do I sign for this man?"

It was all over and it was just beginning.

"That was one of the most unforgettable moments of my life," Dave said, "to see that banker with no more 'buts' and Kenny standing up for me. Why did he do it? He knew me. *That's* the people business."

POPEYE'S RESTAURANT

In 1963, Dave and Laura Longaberger began the restaurant business with very little stock left over and $135. One of Dave's younger brothers, Gary, recalls helping Dave and Laura paint and fix up the restaurant. He also helped out by loaning Dave about $200. It seems that Dave forgot to pay Gary back, until Gary shared his story of helping Dave out at Bee '92. True to form, Dave asked Gary to join him on stage. Dave reached into his pocket, pulled out two crisp one hundred dollar bills, gave them to Gary and said, "Here's your money. I don't want to hear this story again!" Gary broke into laughter and the Bee audience loved it.

Although most restaurants would buy from suppliers, Dave couldn't afford to buy a case of anything. So he drove to the corner grocery every morning and bought five pounds of hamburger, a couple of heads of lettuce and cabbage, half a dozen tomatoes and two cans of vegetables and fruits.

> **BUD CONFIRMED FOR DAVE THAT IF YOU PROVIDE QUALITY AND SERVICE, CUSTOMERS WILL RETURN.**

They would serve lunch, take inventory, take the money made from lunch and buy supper. This continued for several months. They were then able to buy from a wholesaler. "I would still recommend this method to anyone wanting to get in the restaurant or grocery business," Dave said.

Dave and Laura worked day and night for that first year. Then Laura was able to return to her nursing career. At this time Dave thought, "I'm doing okay in the restaurant business, but I know I can do better. I need someone with restaurant experience to advise me. I wonder if my competition will help me out?"

Unheard of? Almost. But it had worked once already for Dave during his bread route days. Is it a valid technique? Perhaps it's a judgment call involving a variety of variables peculiar to each situation. Or perhaps you just ask and see what happens.

One of the best restaurants in the county was Halls' Brown Cow, 16 miles south of Dresden in Zanesville. It was owned and operated by Bud and Florence Hall.

Dave called Bud and told him that he needed help. Bud said yes. Ironically, Dave's competitor soon became his mentor.

Bud confirmed for Dave that if you provide quality and service, customers will return. He also gave him a formula. "If you keep your labor at 18% and your food at 45%, you'll make money."

Bud also encouraged Dave to join the Ohio State Restaurant Association. Dave was able to learn from these members as well. "No matter what your business is, join the industry association. Listen to them because at least collectively, they know more than you do. You can't do it alone. Don't be a fool and think otherwise."

"It was at this point in my life that I learned I had to depend on others and couldn't do everything myself. I thought if I was strong, firm and fair, I didn't need anyone else. But I couldn't have kept my business without people like Laura, Ula and Herman Eschman (Laura's parents), Kenny Martin and Bud and Florence Hall.

"So with my new-found wisdom I immediately made a pretty big error. I named our restaurant the Midway Dairy Bar. I thought this was brilliant because it was midway between Zanesville and Coshocton, Ohio. Well, everyone thought it was a brilliant idea . . . except for everyone."

Dave heard people adamantly call the dairy bar "Popeye's" and he would consistently correct them. "It's the Midway." "Who wants to go to a Midway?" they would ask.

Dave learned they wanted to go to Popeye's. They liked Popeye and wanted to go see him. Dave learned at least three things that helped him immeasurably in later years:

1) Don't be afraid to admit a mistake.
2) Don't underestimate the power of your name.
3) Listen to what your customers want.

Dave's new response was, "If it makes you happy and me money, I'm happy!" It became Popeye's Dairy Bar.

POPEYE'S GROWS

Dave decided that as long as the name was changed to Popeye's, he should have fun with it.

POPEYE'S AFTER EXPANSION (1966)

He knew that his marketing ideas would excite the kids and that parents would go where their children led them. "I learned a great deal about merchandising then," Dave surmised.

The business continued to grow and Dave expanded the restaurant. At the time, his business consisted of adults at lunch and kids the rest of the time. During the remodeling, Dave noticed that the number of teens was declining, but his receipts were increasing. He also noticed that adults were buying more and that more adults were coming in. He decided to investigate.

He didn't solve the mystery until the remodeling was completed. The workmen wanted to know if he was ready to put the *jukebox* back in. That was the reason! Dave had no idea a missing jukebox was affecting his customer demographics and increasing revenue. "We never put the jukebox back in. I also learned to pay more attention to environment in the workplace."

Not only was the Longaberger business growing, but also the Longaberger family. Rachel was born in 1967.

IT'S OKAY TO HAVE A GOOD TIME... AT WORK?

Dave noticed the laughter in the restaurant seemed to correspond to repeat business. "By accident, I seemed to have waitresses who had a terrific sense of humor, and the customers loved it. Some of the waitresses would play jokes on me, tell customers jokes and even sit down and talk to the customers if they had time. The customers loved it and came back for more.

"I do believe that's where a lot of restaurants and stores make a mistake. They need to hire service personnel with a sense of humor, who can roll with the punches. Pay them a little more. I guarantee you, you'll get it back in repeat business.

"In my case, good waitresses with a terrific sense of humor made our restaurant. I believe without it, they can break your business. They are the ones who project who and what the restaurant (or your business) is. You don't need all these dumb training programs that are floating around. Just hire caring people with a sense of humor and everything else will fall into place."

Dave was quite a prankster himself. "I didn't pull any jokes on people unless I knew they had a good sense of humor," he disclaimed. It was more of an effort to show the fun side of the business and life. Consider the following:

Dave sometimes served a rubber hot dog, complete with mustard and ketchup to an unsuspecting customer.

Then there was the plastic ice cube with the fly in it.

"I also used to have one of those rubber suction things that I put between a coffee cup and a saucer. When the customer picked up the cup, the saucer went with it. This was a riot! Most of them would look around to see if anyone was watching and would try to pry the cup (full of coffee) off the saucer. A few would pick both up and try to act natural."

One of Dave's favorite jokes was his invisible ink. A woman happened to sit by the cash register one day and asked Dave if he liked her new sweater. "Yes, it's very nice," he said as he was putting ink on the cash register pad. Then he squirted some ("a pretty big squirt") on her new sweater. "You had to be there, I guess. I thought this lady was going to come over the counter for me being so clumsy. I told her I would pay to have it cleaned. She said it couldn't be cleaned. I said I'd buy her a new sweater. She said she didn't want a new sweater. While she was still fuming, she looked down to survey the damage again and the ink was gone. She thought it was funny. Again, I only did that type of thing with people I knew pretty well. She did get me back. I just can't tell it in this book."

"Dad worked behind the grill," Tami Longaberger recalled. "He bought the food, served the customers and took the garbage to the dump. He worked hard, but he had fun in the process.

"When I was 14 and Rachel was eight, we spent quite a bit of time at Popeye's. I would take Rachel's order and serve her at the counter."

"I particularly enjoyed making my own ice cream cone," Rachel Longaberger Schmidt added. "That was almost as much fun as watching Tami get hit in the face with a pie."

"Dad and I were challenging each other," Tami laughed. "Dad said, 'You better watch it or I'll put a pie in your face!' I told him, 'I bet you won't do it.'"

Dave continued the story. "Before she got 'won't' out, she had pie in her face."

EMPLOYEE MOTIVATION

Dave thought it was important to keep his employees excited about their jobs. He let them participate in menu planning. He used their ideas for new products. He also would ask them to tabulate the sales for the day. "This was a motivator," Dave said. "If they saw the business did $200 for breakfast compared with yesterday's $160, they got excited and motivated to make tomorrow's receipts higher than today's. They had a goal, something more than just a paycheck."

QUALITY

Popeye's Dairy Bar competed with nine other eating places. Its prices were 25% higher than the others and still commanded the largest share of customers. Besides the customer service, Dave emphasized quality.

"We were the cleanest restaurant in town. I liked to wash the dishes myself and people liked knowing that. They knew when they came into our restaurant, at least they wouldn't catch anything they didn't have when they walked in."

They also developed the reputation for having the freshest food and even the best cup of coffee. Although many thought of it as wasteful, Dave threw coffee out after 20 minutes. "I do believe a good cup of coffee is one of the main draws. I insisted on throwing ours out after 20 minutes. People do not mind waiting if you say you have a pot brewing. I love to walk into a restaurant and see two customers and six pots of coffee getting old. I've been in some restaurants where I thought the coffee was old enough to vote. I learned that it was worth the money to get the reputation."

POPEYE'S EXPANDS...SORT OF

As the restaurant grew, Dave wanted to expand to other cities. "I realized that there were 1,500 people in Dresden and 235 million people outside of Dresden."

COSHOCTON, OHIO, POPEYE'S
"A FLASH OF STUPIDITY"

Dave reasoned if he could do this well in Dresden with so few people, the larger the town, the larger the revenue. "I went to Coshocton, a town 15 times larger than Dresden. I was half-cocked. Six months later I came back with my tail between my legs.

"I surprised myself that I could truly encounter stupidity in such a dramatic way. But I learned a business needs people, products and systems. It has to have all three. My problem in Coshocton was that I didn't have the people, the products or the system. I didn't have the right personalities. The food wasn't as good as it could have been. I didn't have the time there and didn't train others to create the needed atmosphere. That was a true flash of stupidity."

Although Dresden's Popeye's was continuing to do business, Dave had lost so much money in the other restaurant it was like starting all over again.

He laid off a few employees and did everything himself, from washing the windows to the dishes to making the ice cream to waiting and busing tables. Within eight months he had recovered, but "It was an education I'll always carry with me. I learned again that you can be aggressive and cautious. You always need an insurance plan, someone on the bank to save you."

SEEING A NEED

In 1968, five years after Popeye's had begun, Dave saw an opportunity. The A&P Grocery was closing. Dave needed more space. Perhaps he could use the 4,000 square foot grocery store as a restaurant. He approached Bob Matthews, the owner, about a $9,000 land contract, on monthly payments. Bob said yes. Dave then approached A&P about buying some of their equipment for the buffet. They said he could have it all for $2,800. He didn't need it all unless . . . well, come to think of it, Dresden needed a good grocery store.

So Dave applied the LTD system to it. There was an obvious need. He had the experience. But once again he didn't have the money for stock. What could he do? First, would A&P set up payments for the $2,800?

**WHEN DAVE FIRST BOUGHT THE A&P GROCERY,
HE CALLED IT POPEYE'S FOOD STORE.**

Yes. Could he go to the bank to get a loan? "The banker still hid from me," Dave recounted.

Through some more strategizing, Dave remembered that Fairmont Dairy had approached him about financing some badly needed restaurant equipment in return for his restaurant exclusively purchasing their dairy products. Dave refused out of loyalty to Kenny Martin.

Dave eventually countered. Would they finance grocery stock? They said yes in return for selling their products in the grocery. Dave said, "As long as Kenny Martin's dairy also gets space." Dave had learned the importance of remembering those who had helped him in the past.

Longaberger was now in the grocery business. It was soon qualified to be the Dresden IGA Foodliner. Although its first weeks were nominal, the grocery soon was one of the most profitable businesses in town.

"The Dresden IGA Foodliner was exciting and different from the restaurant but it was also the same," Dave said. "Fifty percent was people. I was in charge of the people. Thirty percent was good products.

I chose the best products. Twenty percent was the system. IGA was in charge of the books, the specials and grocery training. Little did I know that this experience was to play a major part in the structure of Longaberger Baskets.

"It was the same as with the restaurant business. It's as simple as that. This is the main ingredient of any business. You've got to know your labor and material costs."

Since Dave was always in the grocery, people looked for him. He talked to the customers and to their children. He told jokes. He still played jokes, like slipping dog food in a customer's basket who didn't have a dog. "They would have the strangest expression on their faces when they saw that can of dog food in the check out line," Dave laughed. "It got to the point where customers expected me to joke with them and if I didn't, they thought I was mad.

"Actually, I found it much harder to entertain in the grocery store than in the restaurant. But I knew it could be done."

One of the consistencies Dave found in service industries was the front line personnel, whether they were waitresses, cashiers, clerks or

THE DRESDEN IGA AFTER SOME IMPROVEMENTS.

Sales Consultants. "Many times you might have a terrific butcher, a terrific dairy person, produce person and beverage person, but the check out clerk controls the mood of the customers when they leave the store.

"One time we had a check out clerk who everyone would talk to. I noticed that the line was always pretty long at her check out stand. I could never figure out why until I stopped to watch. The customer would come up and Betty said, 'Hi, how are you?' and they started talking. As a matter of fact, many customers waited in line just to give an answer to her question.

"She probably brought in customers. Maybe supermarkets shouldn't worry so much about how fast customers get in and out, but more about the clerks and cashiers interacting with the customers. They should worry less about how many they check out and more about how many they bring back. Bottom line: you need up-front people with good personalities who enjoy their jobs."

Dave continued to expand the grocery store, added a drug store and also managed the restaurant. The sole purpose of the drug store was so that Dresden would have one. Dave sold it shortly after he initiated it. "I didn't know anything about a drugstore. I just knew we needed one."

THE DRESDEN IGA AFTER FINAL IMPROVEMENTS.

During this time, Tami began working as a hostess at the restaurant on Sundays for the after-church crowd. She worked two nights a week at the drug store. She later switched to work at the grocery store.

"Some of our worst arguments happened over Tami going to work," Dave said. "It was a real challenge to get Tami to go to work. But once she got there, she did a good job and customers would come up and say, 'Isn't it nice that she wants to work?' As a father of a teenage daughter, I controlled my thoughts."

"I *had* to work," Tami said. "When I was 16, I wanted a really neat car. But, I ended up getting a 1973 Mercury Caprice. I told Dad that I could drive a manual transmission and talked him into making the down payment. When we got in the car in downtown Zanesville, he saw that I couldn't operate the clutch. He was so mad! When we got home, he made me drive up and back on our tiny driveway ten times! I had to make the monthly payments so I had to work."

Meanwhile, Rachel began working as a cashier at the drug store at the ripe old age of ten. Even before that, she worked at the restaurant, separating coffee filters and pre-measuring coffee in the filters.

LONGABERGER BASKETS BUFFET: OUTSIDE

In the early '70s, the restaurant was generating about $4,000 a week. The grocery was doing about $20,000 a week, for a combined profit of about $1,000 per week, before taxes, a handsome sum in the early '70s.

"I knew there was something else for me to do. I knew I could not sit on my experience and knowledge. It just didn't feel right. But what else was there for me to do?"

> **"MAYBE SUPERMARKETS SHOULDN'T WORRY SO MUCH ABOUT HOW FAST CUSTOMERS GET IN AND OUT, BUT MORE ABOUT THE CLERKS AND CASHIERS INTERACTING WITH THE CUSTOMERS. THEY SHOULD WORRY LESS ABOUT HOW MANY THEY CHECK OUT AND MORE ABOUT HOW MANY THEY BRING BACK."**

A LECTURE ON WHEELS

"Going anywhere with Dad was a learning opportunity, and Rachel and I were his captive audience," Tami recalled.

"We called it a *Lecture on Wheels*," Rachel added.

"He would begin with, 'Now, I'm going to tell you this because you need to hear it,' and we would look at each other and sigh," Tami said. "He usually made a good point."

A FORK IN THE ROAD...WHICH WAY?

I suppose we all have forks in the road. There are plateaus in all of our lives when we can continue what we're doing or go a separate way. It could be moving to a different part of the country. It could be working for a new company. It could be getting married. Or divorced. It might be starting a new profession. It could be creating your own business.

LONGABERGER BASKETS BUFFET: INSIDE

It's been said some of us don't see the forest for the trees. I wonder if that's like opportunity. Could it be that some of us don't recognize opportunity until it's too late? It's easy to see opportunity after the fact. The trick is seeing it while it's still opportunity.

Meanwhile, back in Dresden in the early '70s, Dave was still being told he was doing things the wrong way. For example, he was told that he shouldn't let his employees know how much the business was making. "They said, 'Popeye, if you ever want to make any money in this town, don't show people that you're making any money.' I didn't believe that. The critics' problem was they weren't putting any of their money back in the business. So, I continued putting it back where people could see we used better equipment or better landscaping or more merchandise. I gave the employees the freedom to check the cash register because I wanted them to think of it as their business too."

> **IT'S EASY TO SEE OPPORTUNITY AFTER THE FACT. THE TRICK IS SEEING IT WHILE IT'S STILL OPPORTUNITY.**

With the store and restaurant operating as planned, Dave began actively seeking new opportunities. He saw a need for an independent restaurant alliance. He visited ten restaurants in the area. He asked what they paid for their merchandise and found inconsistencies. Restaurants were paying different prices for the same merchandise from the same vendor. There was a need for fair and consistent pricing to the independent restaurant owner, so Dave created the Independent Restaurant Association.

In his travels, Dave would walk through the new malls to discover new ideas. It was there he discovered a new trend that touched his heart like no other product. He noticed basket displays in several stores. He would stop, pick up a basket and smile as he thought back to an earlier time. As he would look at the basket he would think, "Dad's baskets are ten times better quality than these wicker things."

He began to ask the clerks how the sales were going and found out they were becoming very popular. He also thought, "But like everything else, foreign baskets are so cheap, they'd be hard to compete with." So he let the idea go and went back to pursuing the restaurant association. But the baskets would not leave his mind.

That's usually a good sign, isn't it? If an idea won't leave *you* alone, you'd better investigate! There aren't too many things in life you'll find that you can put your hands and heart into.

> AS HE WOULD LOOK AT THE BASKET HE WOULD THINK, "DAD'S BASKETS ARE TEN TIMES BETTER QUALITY THAN THESE WICKER THINGS."

Dave thought, "The only way to find out is to *do* it."

Dave went to his father in 1972. J.W. had closed his shop in 1955. Dave knew that his father still made a basket every now and then and asked if he'd give him a dozen. Dave took them to Roscoe Village, a restored canal town a few miles away in Coshocton. He found a turn-of-the-century general store and said, "I'll sell this basket to you for five dollars on consignment if you'll sell it for $9.95." The store sold them instantly and wanted more.

So Dave went to his father and said, "Dad, could you make me ten dozen of those medium market baskets? I'll pay you five dollars each." Dave's father was selling them for the same price he'd always sold them for, $1.50, and thought Dave had been working too hard. "He thought I was nuts!"

Dave wasn't interested in the money for this fact-finding mission. He wanted to see if people would buy the baskets for ten dollars. The ten dozen baskets sold in a month.

Now comes the fork in the road.

LONGABERGER BASKETS ...A NEW BIRTH

As the basket business was beginning with a flourish, tragedy struck. J.W. Longaberger died of a heart attack at 71 years of age.

More than ever, Dave felt the desire to continue the family tradition. But he didn't want to make the baskets himself. As Dave explains:

"As a kid, I was not crazy about making baskets. I worked with Dad some making the bottoms, but my love was working on Main Street, the corner store, the restaurant and the movie house. Through sports, the

DAVE'S FIRST BASKET SHOP — J.W.'S HANDWOVEN BASKETS

army, working on a bread truck, running the restaurant and the grocery store. I learned the arts of managing, marketing and merchandising. It was laid out for me.

"I believe it's laid out for you too. Look close at your past and present."

With his father's death and his brothers and sisters in their own professions and lives, Dave needed weavers. So he bought a small building on a "land contract" across the street from his restaurant and hired Kenny Birkhimer, the first employee of the company and Bonnie Hague (Kenny's sister). Then the number increased to five weavers. Dave's brother Larry shared his basket making knowledge with the first weavers.

Snow came in the windows and ceiling as those early weavers created Longaberger Baskets. There was no heat and no bathroom. They had to use the company truck to get to the restaurant's bathroom.

"Back in Dresden, with no outside help, we were on our own. The mistakes were to be our teachers."

Dave asked himself three questions:

1) *Will people buy the baskets*? There was an obvious demand although he didn't have a way to measure it. He just knew the baskets they made were selling.

2) *Could people make the baskets*? Yes, and they were getting better at it every day.

3) *Was the material available*? Dave found that it was.

THE HARTVILLE CONNECTION

One of the first things that Dave had to do was to find a source of material. He located a veneering plant in Hartville, Ohio, The Aspen Basket Company. There, Dave met Charles Kimberly, the owner, who agreed to veneer on the weekends for Longaberger Baskets. Dave would drive up each weekend and bring the splints back, spread them out and let them dry.

"Dave told me what he wanted to do and asked if I would do some veneering for him on the weekends," Mr. Kimberly remembered. "He told me that he was just beginning the basket business and I liked him from the start. All I furnished was the lathe operator and the clipper operator (to cut the sheets of wood into splints). Dave brought his help from Dresden and they worked all day Saturday and Sunday to get the splints out."

The weavers soon became more adept. Dave added a space heater (although they still wore their coats and gloves), a picnic table to eat on and a port-a-let bathroom outside.

From 1973 to 1977, Dave did a lot of experimenting and observing with the marketing of the baskets. It became clear that the baskets could be made with a high level of quality. It was also clear that the demand for baskets was continuing to increase.

CHARLES KIMBERLY

While Tami and Rachel watched, Dave constructed the first Longaberger Baskets display in the grocery store. Customers could simply put one of the baskets on the display in their shopping carts and buy it.

Did the display generate sales? "No," Dave laughed.

FIRST LONGABERGER BASKETS DISPLAY, 1974.

"Sales were not satisfying in the shops," Dave said. "I knew there was something missing. We had a good product and the weavers enjoyed making them, but something had to be done to sell more baskets."

Dave was forced to pull some of the weavers to market the baskets. It was hard to balance production and sales. Sales continued to climb, however, and Dave needed more room.

THE OLD WOOLEN MILL BECOMES NEW LONGABERGER PLANT

Dave looked around town and didn't see anything that interested him until he thought about the old woolen mill where his mother used to work. It was plenty big, 34,000 square feet big. The only problem was, it had been vacant since 1955, about 20 years.

Dave decided to drive over and take a look. For most potential tenants, one look would be all it took. As he waded through the weeds to peek through a broken window pane, he forgot all about the possibility of being snake bitten. He saw that part of the roof had caved in. Every window was broken or boarded up. Trees were growing right up through the rotted floor and what ceiling there was. Several walls had also collapsed. It doesn't exactly sound like a real estate cover piece. But Dave was excited. Through that broken out window, he could see hundreds of people weaving, staining, tacking, laughing and talking. For 20 years, the old woolen mill was seen as a memorial to the American past – the factory. Dave saw the future in that same broken down building.

Dave visited owner Richard Johnson in Coshocton, and explained he wanted to buy the building on a land contract. That is, Dave would make the factory usable and would make monthly payments. The worst that could happen was that Dave would not be successful, but that Mr. Johnson would still have a much improved, more marketable building. "They liked the basket idea," Dave recalled. "I gave them a bunch of baskets. Mr. Johnson said for the price of $7,000 in back taxes, it was mine." Dave would pay $200 per month until it was paid off.

THE OLD WOOLEN MILL AFTER DAVE BOUGHT IT.

A lot of people thought Dave was crazy. He said, "I did it *my way,* not somebody else's. I didn't tell anyone else my ideas until I was sold on them and even then I usually went ahead and did them before I told very many. If I succeeded or failed, I wanted it to be my way or I knew I wouldn't be happy."

Dave spent his weekends working on the old woolen mill, soon to become Plant One. "We burned the collapsed roof right in the building," Dave recalled. "It was great practice for the fire department."

How did Tami and Rachel react when they learned that Dave purchased the woolen mill?

"We were less than excited," Rachel responded. "Teenagers always think their parents are an embarrassment. Dad was always doing something that was highly embarrassing to us, like hanging a rubber chicken from his antenna and driving through town. But this was the worst.

"One day, my friends and I heard fire truck sirens. Because there wasn't much other entertainment to choose from, we hopped on our bicycles and followed the trucks to the woolen mill. Dad was standing in front of the building with his arms folded.

> **FOR 20 YEARS THE OLD WOOLEN MILL WAS SEEN AS A MEMORIAL TO THE AMERICAN PAST — THE FACTORY. DAVE SAW THE FUTURE IN THAT SAME BROKEN DOWN BUILDING.**

"I thought, *Oh, No! He bought this place!* I rode through the firemen and their hoses up to Dad. You have to understand that this was the most dilapidated building in Dresden. I asked him if he bought it.

"He said, 'Yeah, we're burning it out.'

"What could he possibly make out of that building! I thought he had spent all of his money and I was going to an orphanage."

He cleaned, hammered, insulated and improvised until he had room for his growing basket company. Dave remembered an early episode at the new building:

"I was explaining to the weavers (by now, 15 in number) how to make a certain type of basket. I was rattling on like I had made hundreds. I had never made this basket or hardly any baskets. My job as a kid was to make bottoms, when Dad could catch me.

"Well, every basket has its own little secret. I was explaining those secrets to them when I stopped. Where is that information coming from? I knew I didn't know how to make that basket. I turned and looked over my right shoulder, and to this day it still gives me goose pimples. There was an image of Dad from his waist up. I have never seen my father since. Evidently we're doing a good job.

"I have been asked many times, 'Wouldn't it be wonderful if your Dad could see what has happened to his baskets?' My answer to that is 'he does.' "

As the demand for splints increased, Dave bought the Aspen Basket Company in Hartville from Mr. Kimberly. Through a land contract and a handshake he agreed to purchase what became known as Plant Two.

Rachel began working during the summers at the plant, beginning about age 14. She continued to ride her bike to work.

"I parked my bike right next to Aunt Carmen's," she laughed.

Her first job was to cut strips of paper and stamp them. This served as the product tag. She also worked the early shift (6:00 a.m. to 2:30 p.m.) when needed. "That was *hard work*! It's helped me be more sensitive to employee burnout. It's why I appreciate employees who have worked for Longaberger for years and years. It's helped me understand a little better the motivation they need on a regular basis. I think it's why I've always understood the importance of the Human Resources department, incentives and health care."

Tami's tenure, on the other hand, did not last quite as long. "The first day, I worked eight hours in the forming department," Tami laughed. "The next day I worked four hours and got a three hour lecture from Dad when I told him I wanted to move into sales. But I went with him to a basket show that night. That was my first show."

WELCOME TO THE PARTY!

Charleen Cuckovich and her family were out for a Sunday drive when they stopped in a small Amish shop in Ohio. Being a basket collector, Charleen immediately looked around and happened upon a shelf of dusty baskets. "It was love at first sight," Charleen said. "I couldn't believe the (low) prices! I wanted to know all about them, like where they were made and who made them."

The store's owner said they were made by a man named Longaberger who lived in Dresden. "I told my family that I wanted to go to Dresden. I guess they could tell that I *really* wanted to go, and off we went. I finally saw this little town and it seemed like all the houses were painted white and all of the porches had flowers. It was just the way I hoped it would look."

Charleen and her family searched all over for the basket plant and finally saw an old mill with a basket hanging from the porch. "That's it!" Charleen chirped. She asked her husband to go inside and inquire if they could watch.

Charleen's husband came back with a big smile. "They said it's fine. You're going to *love* this place!"

So Charleen and her family walked up to the porch and saw three sets of hand prints in the concrete: Dave's and two little sets: Tami and Rachel's. Inside, they saw several weavers making baskets. Their workroom was small and rustic. Baskets were nailed on the walls, a picnic table was in the corner and the weaving "horse" was in the middle of the room.

They seemed pleased that Charleen was so interested in their work and were delighted to answer her questions. "I was in seventh heaven," Charleen remembered. "I think we stayed there all afternoon." She asked one of the weavers if she could have the basket she just finished. When the happy weaver obliged and handed her the basket, Charleen asked her to sign it. A tradition was born that continues today.

Charleen bought a van load of baskets for $200 and immediately planned to build a log cabin close to their home in which to sell the baskets. As they headed home, Charleen climbed in the back to admire each of her baskets. The year was 1978. A new chapter was being written in the Longaberger Story.

While Charleen thought about how to sell the baskets, she called her friends and said, "Come right over! You've got to see these baskets I found." When her friends saw them, they wanted some of their own. She began to get calls from her friends, "Tell me about how these baskets were made and what was that man's name again?"

It hit her. Sell the baskets in homes where you can tell the story of how they're made. So she kept selling them and ordering more. One day, however, she was told she would not be able to purchase any more baskets. Dave wasn't sure how he wanted to sell them and was putting a freeze on selling them to outside vendors.

"I was heartbroken," Charleen recalled. "I didn't know what to do." She tried to get in touch with Dave, whom she'd never met. Finally, she did and they arranged a meeting for the next week.

Charleen and her husband met with Dave and another couple. It was decided that baskets were selling better in the homes than in the stores. "As soon as I heard about having a basket party in someone's home, I knew this was it," Dave said. "The idea hit me like an explosion."

Charleen has been with the company ever since. "Charleen was a fireball, full of ideas and energy. We both held parties and the response was better than I ever hoped for. We told them about the history of the baskets and my family. And, the more we told them, the more they wanted to know. They were interested in my family of 12 brothers and sisters, my mother, what she did now, how many weavers we had, how long it takes them to weave a basket, and on and on."

Charleen said the basket parties were like a time machine. "They took a step back in time to a more calm and peaceful era, when your neighbors had time to talk to you and families ate together and everyone sat on the front porch and talked. We told them about the old time uses of the baskets and many would just nod their heads because they could remember."

> **"AS SOON AS I HEARD ABOUT HAVING A BASKET PARTY IN SOMEONE'S HOME, I KNEW THIS WAS IT," DAVE SAID. "THE IDEA HIT ME LIKE AN EXPLOSION."**

The basket parties were setting a mood for the customers to associate the baskets with the aesthetics of days gone by, quality of workmanship and decorative and useful applications.

"Because we didn't have a catalog," Tami said, "the Consultants had to carry all the baskets for customers to see. It wasn't an official rule, but Dad strongly suggested that Consultants get a van or truck."

Marge Shipley, one of the first Consultants, recalls, "I took over 100 baskets to each show."

Soon afterwards, the baskets were pulled from the store shelves never to become dusty again.

MORE GROWING PAINS

The basket business was growing fast but so were the bills. Dave was funding it with his other businesses, and money was getting tight. "I did not want stockholders or politicians or the mafia. I knew they'd all be smarter than me, so I couldn't let them in."

But year by year, more and more money was going to pay for salaries, supplies, rent and utilities. And sometimes not everyone got paid. That's why the IRS came to the Dresden Plant with a chain and padlock. As Dave recounted, "He came. A short, mean-looking man. (I didn't want to say he was ugly, he might still work for the IRS.) I almost died when he showed up, but I told myself, 'I don't care, I'm going to give it one last try.'

"I took him through the plant. I showed him everything: where we came from, where we are and where we're headed. He didn't change his expression. I laid all my books out. He looked it all over. After an hour and a half, he said, 'Mr. Longaberger, there is no reason why the bank shouldn't give you the money to pay us.' I don't know what I was expecting, but it sure wasn't that! I blurted out 'Will you call the banker and tell him what you just told me?' He had me sign a permission slip and he called."

> **"I DIDN'T WANT TO SAY HE WAS UGLY, HE MIGHT STILL WORK FOR THE IRS."**

The next day, Dave received a call from a bank president in Zanesville who said that Dave shouldn't have asked the IRS to call him for a loan to pay his taxes. He laughed and said, "You just don't do things like that."

Dave said, "I do. Are you going to give me the loan?"

"No."

But from past experience, Dave felt that the IRS would set up a payment plan if no one else would give him credit.

No one else did. The IRS set up a payment plan. "I'm thankful that they did. I think it's ironic that I've had better transactions with the IRS than with banks. Banks have almost put me out of business. The IRS helped look for a way to keep me in. In a way, they were like Dad; they gave me another chance."

But Dave's problems weren't over. The basket business was still draining his finances. Two years later, Dave attended a meeting at his restaurant with a few farmers to hear Jack Hill from the Ohio Farm Bureau. After the meeting, Dave showed him the baskets. Jack got excited. "Dave, this is what the American Dream is all about!"

"Good. Jack, I need some money."

As a matter of fact, he needed a lot of money. He was in debt for $400,000: $100,000 to suppliers, $175,000 to the IRS, $75,000 to McLean's Grocery and $50,000 to the lumber company. Dave had also just separated from Laura, Tami and Rachel.

This was one of the worst times of Dave Longaberger's life. "I knew the baskets were to be great someday, because every year our sales were going up and our labor cost was going down. I knew there would be a payday but it seemed like all of the money was still not quite enough. I knew the future was going to be good if I could just keep things afloat.

"With that in mind, I would go home at night to my little apartment after a hard day at three jobs. I would be so depressed and I worked hard not to show it to my employees. But there in my empty apartment I was very dejected. Strange as it may sound, about the only way I made it was through Frank Sinatra's song, 'My Way.' I would lie on the floor and play it ten or 15 times. Then I would go to sleep. Sleep was my escape."

Dave was able to get a loan. That was the good news. The bad news was he had to put up the deeds to Popeye's, the grocery store, the basket shop and his home.

Dave then did something that seemed inappropriate. He took a vacation. He owed over $400,000 and he took his very first vacation.

"I went to Mexico and I thought I would not be able to lie on the beach for seven days. I went and I don't think I moved. When I came back, I was so full of energy! There was no problem I could not face. If you can afford it, go. You cannot afford not to go in situations like this.

"Finally, with the loan approved, the bills paid, I said, 'Let's get the show on the road! We're ready to jump on this like ugly on an ape.'"

In 1979, there were 30 Consultants and 40 employees. In 1980, there were 50 Consultants and 70 employees. The old woolen mill housed manufacturing, processing, shipping and sales.

Dave decided to expand his restaurant to seat 164 customers. As Dave explains, "About 1978, I had another flash of stupidity. I could see tourists come to Dresden to visit our basket plant.

"By 1980, my payments were $10,000 a month for the loan. The recession hit and tourists didn't come. My loan went from 8% to 23% on a $400,000 loan! That forced me to sell my restaurant.

"I could never understand why the bank didn't refinance the loan to me. They just came in and sold it to a family with no business experience at all, let alone restaurant experience. Plus, they extended the loan from ten to 15 years at a lower interest rate.

"That was my first love. I cried for two days. I knew I would get it back some day and, sure enough, almost 25 years from the day we bought it from Harry, we bought it back from the same bank that forced us to sell it."

THE TEST OF THE '80s

Little did Dave realize what was lurking around the corner. It seems that just when one fire was put out, another one popped up. But the lessons of the past had tutored him on how to cope with adversity. "The next few years would be a test of my strength, firmness and fairness."

It began with the growing organizational pains many businesses have experienced. Dave saw problems in the sales field organization. Territories weren't respected. Some of the sales Consultants had more privileges than others. Dave wanted more uniformity and control. "I wanted a Sales Consultant in New York and one in L.A. to have the same type of hostess programs, customer specials, incentives and commissions. It was getting too complicated and too out of control.

"We instituted a new sales program. Two of our distributors hired attorneys during the litigation to follow and I had to talk to their attorneys. I wasn't used to that and will never get used to that. I want to talk to the people I'm dealing with. After a few weeks, and against the instructions of everyone's attorneys, I called them up and said, 'I'm tired of talking to the third person. You don't like our new plan so I'll give you $1,000 for each Consultant you have and have you paid off in a year.'

"Since they thought our company would never survive our new plan, they agreed to it. Of course, their attorneys almost went into cardiac arrest. Incidentally, we paid them off in six months."

THE WORLD'S LARGEST HEADACHE

That same year, 1981, manufacturing was ahead of sales for the first time. To enhance sales, Dave and his employees built "The World's Largest Basket." It was actually begun as a float for the Dresden Homecoming Parade and as Tami remembers, "It soon got out of hand." Dave decided to take it to the Ohio State Fair. It was large enough to walk through and see basket displays inside.

In 16 days, 500 basket parties were booked and 80 new Consultants were signed. The problem was, there were only 25 Consultants in Columbus. In other words, there was no way for 25 Consultants to handle 500 parties or 80 recruits. "What a lesson we learned!" Dave lamented. "If you don't learn anything else from my mistake, learn this: when you come up with a plan, come up with a follow through."

And remember that Dave was paying off his $400,000 loan at 23% interest. Anyone care for an aspirin? Better take it now before you hear what happened next!

THE WORLD'S "LARGEST PICNIC BASKET," MADE FROM FIVE
MAPLE TREES, MEASURING NINE FEET WIDE, 27 FEET LONG AND
TEN FEET HIGH. THE HANDLES WERE 23 FEET OFF THE GROUND.

PROBLEMS, PROBLEMS, PROBLEMS

Dave was hit with a barrage of simultaneous problems. Because of his concern for laid off employees, he decided to run a special on one of the largest and most time consuming baskets. He offered the $100 hamper basket at 75% off. Although still losing money, Dave knew the cash flow could stand it if they sold 8,000 but no more.

"I knew we would only sell 8,000, but we sold 20,000." That caused a severe cash flow problem, since it took so long to fill the orders. To offset one sale, Longaberger was forced to offer another. So they offered the magazine basket special, expecting to sell 24,000. Instead, they sold 44,000 baskets at 35% off. The hole was getting deeper, forcing them to offer another special. This time it was a corn basket, and instead of selling the anticipated 20,000, they sold 120,000 at 50% off!

To meet such demands, Longaberger had to hire 500 extra weavers to get the orders out by Christmas. They had to open a new plant in Millersburg to house the operation. At that moment not only was the rug pulled out from under Dave, the whole plant was.

In February 1983, the Hartville veneering plant, Plant Two, was destroyed by fire. The insurance was almost nil. As Mr. Kimberly remembers, "I was on vacation when they called and told me, and I was devastated. I had never signed any papers with Dave and I knew he was just beginning to get started with his basket business. He called me as soon as he could get hold of me and said, 'Kim, this was my fire; it wasn't yours. As far as I'm concerned, our deal is just as good as it was before the fire.'

"We had only about $20,000 in insurance which covered maybe three percent of what we needed. But Dave said, 'Okay, you take the insurance money.' I thought this was a wonderful thing. He said, 'Kim, what would you really like to have?' I said, 'Well, Dave, if I had my druthers, I don't suppose you can do this, but I'd like to have $3,000 a month for 15 years.' He turned to his attorneys and said, 'That's what he wants. Figure it out so he can have it.' That's what we've gotten. He's never been late, even though things were mighty, mighty tough."

Both of the lathes were destroyed, 30,000 square feet of building was a total loss. The only salvageable item in the entire plant was the boiler. Dave formed his own construction company to rebuild as they could afford it and sometimes when they couldn't.

Years later, Charles Kimberly reflected, "I first met Dave Longaberger in 1979 when he came to my factory to ask me to cut some veneer for him. The amount of business he brought wasn't large, and we wouldn't normally have deviated from business as usual to do a favor of this sort. But something about the man told me he was something special and that, at the very least, doing business with him would be enjoyable.

"Still, it was quite a surprise when his business grew rapidly. Two years after I first saw him, he amazed me with an offer to buy my factory. His bankers, however, were less impressed. Now remember that bankers are taught to value only tangible assets. The vision, integrity, drive, and joy of life which were Dave's meant little to bankers. So the only way he could purchase my plant was through 'owner financing', meaning that I would loan him the money.

"Luckily, I had spent a lifetime working with men, and could see the kind of man Dave was. My only risk was that some unforeseen event might destroy his business, and with it, his ability to meet his obligations.

"We worked out a purchase agreement, which included a price. It was strictly an agreement and guaranteed by handshake alone.

"Not long after that, on a Saturday night in 1983, while I was on vacation, disaster struck. A fire destroyed my factory, changing the bulk of my life's savings into a smoldering hulk. Sure, Dave had agreed to buy it, but in fact he had not really, technically done so when it burned to the ground. The next day was one of the worst of my life, as I began canceling my retirement plans, and contemplating a very difficult old age.

"In retrospect, perhaps I panicked, for a moment's clear thought about Dave, about who he was, would have eased my fears. On Monday morning I received a message from him. I don't remember the exact words, but the message was, *We agreed on a closing date, and so from that date forward the factory was mine. That the papers aren't signed is a legal detail. My word is my bond, and takes precedence over such details. The factory was mine. The loss is mine. Have a nice vacation.* Dave

"I'm sure God still makes men like Dave Longaberger. I'm also sure he doesn't make enough."

Meanwhile, Dave had to find a new source for his baskets. He went to the other two veneering plants in Ohio and paid twice the amount he'd been paying. He searched for a veneering manufacturer who would build the half-million dollar lathe on credit. And Dave was already a million dollars in debt.

During this time, the Hartville employees at Plant Two were plenty nervous. Would Dave put another plant in Hartville when he lived 100 miles away in Dresden? It would obviously be a lot easier on him to have the plants in the same city. He built the plant back in Hartville.

GROCERIES OR BASKETS?

In 1983, the fork in the road had finally arrived. Dave had to decide between his grocery business and his basket business. The grocery business had always been very profitable. The basket business had not. The grocery was a very respected business. The basket plant had its skeptics.

In a letter to his employees and Consultants, Dave put his feelings on paper:

I must now sell my only income to keep the basket business alive. There were no second thoughts about it. Every year our labor and material costs are going down and our sales are going up. To meet our bills and make sure everyone got a paycheck, I've sold my IGA store and put the money into our company.

I have heard that there are some folks who think I was foolish for selling two profitable businesses that I worked so hard to build in order to pay the bills for our company which has continued to lose money. Let those folks say what they will. I have faith in our company, in its products and in the people who work here.

I have shown my faith by putting everything that I own into our company and I am confident that I will not be disappointed. Each year in the life of a growing company like ours has special meaning, and the years 1983 and 1984 will be no exception.

The year 1983 has been the most challenging year in our company's history. We have faced many challenges and many hardships together and through hard work and patience, we have overcome them. We have moved ahead and improved Longaberger Baskets in many ways in the face of challenges and hardships in a depressed economy that would have made other people quit.

As you know, our Hartville veneering plant was completely destroyed by fire in February, 1983. Some companies would have closed the Hartville plant, giving up making their own high quality weaving material.

Instead, we rebuilt that plant, installed more modern equipment and further improved the quality of our weaving material. This decision will mean a great deal to the future of our company. Unfortunately for 1983, it meant putting our company further into debt by one million dollars. As most of you know, Longaberger Baskets faced layoffs in the past more often than any of us wanted. When there were not enough basket orders, we just could not operate and employees went without a paycheck.

To keep everyone working this year, we offered a hamper special in February and a magazine basket special in May. Instead of selling the 8,000 hampers that we expected, we sold 20,000 hampers. Instead of selling 24,000 magazine baskets as we expected, we sold 44,000. These sales figures are a credit to all of us and our high quality product.

However, these sales figures, through the specials and tremendous increase in our other sales, meant that we faced the hardships of working on weekends and were forced to expand our operations even more quickly than we had planned. We had to move departments around, open a new plant in Millersburg and hire hundreds of new people.

In 1983, we also faced additional challenges in the financial area. The Hartville fire meant that we had to buy veneer at double our cost to produce it ourselves. Specials meant extra overtime pay and additional shipping expense. The tremendous expense of training so many new people was a substantial investment of time and money.

This has been a challenging year for all of us. Of course, 1983 has not been all hardship. We have had a lot of laughs together and we have continued to see improvements in our plant facilities which make our work days more enjoyable and safer. We have also seen improvements in the size of our paychecks. I am proud of our accomplishments and in our determination to overcome the hardships and frustrations which we have endured.

While there may be many different challenges in the years ahead, the future looks much brighter because of our efforts and determination. By training so many talented new people, we are more prepared than ever to meet the increase in demand from our customers.

We have faced challenges this year, that other people might have run away from, and we won. Let's look forward to 1984 with excitement based on the knowledge of what we have achieved in the difficult days of 1983.

Dave had no insurance policy to fall back on now and he knew it. There was no turning back. There was no one on the bank. This was sink or swim time. But he also knew that someday there would be a payday. The bankers didn't.

"But if push came to shove, I could always go back to managing a restaurant or supermarket or any of my other jobs," Dave said.

DAVE AND THE UNION

By this time, Longaberger Baskets consisted of three plants. Plant One, the old woolen mill, where the weavers were housed. Plant Two, the Hartville veneering plant that was being rebuilt, and Plant Three, the old paper mill which housed the processing departments. His employee count had grown to several hundred and his Consultant count was close to 1,000.

Attempting to bounce back from the recent setbacks, Dave then learned he faced a union organization effort. "I thought, 'This is all I need with the hamper basket problem and the fire!' I got sick because I prided myself on keeping the employees informed of what we were doing now and in the future. But it is amazing how a few employees can sound like the majority." This was an awkward time because Dave was cautioned that anything he said could be used against him.

Dave reasons why the union effort was initiated:

"I was so busy with the fire and sales that I think there was no leadership in manufacturing. The only time you're going to get a union organization is when employees don't trust management. They evidently didn't trust management."

Dave was asked to talk to the employees and his attorneys prepared a four page statement to read. Dave began reading the speech, but the more he read, the madder he got. He threw the speech down and told the employees they had worked too hard to turn it over to a bunch of outsiders. He told them he would do what he had always done, that is, listen to complaints and make corrections as needed. But this wasn't the way to go about it.

"My attorneys just put their heads in their hands. We did get a few complaints but not very many. That was a good signal. After a few months the silent majority spoke up and the union organizers got out of town."

FINANCIAL CRISIS

On April 23, 1986, Dave Longaberger walked into the executive offices and asked, "Where are we?" They looked at the books and saw that they owed their customers five and a half million dollars and owed the IRS about a million and a half dollars.

The day before, on April 22, 1986, Dave had asked Tami and Rachel to his home for a family meeting. As a family, they had decided that bankruptcy was not a viable option.

Dave called an executive meeting of the Vice Presidents and Directors. He presented them with the situation. They could declare bankruptcy or they could try to erase their debts.

Dave made a dramatic decision. The executive team decided to raise the prices by 18%, cut out all specials (which accounted for 40% of their sales), cut the product line from 170 to 70 items and shut down a plant. Dave then called a meeting of the 1,000 employees and apologized. "I'm sorry I let this happen, but I do believe the company can be saved. We're going to have to shut the Millersburg Plant down and lay off half of you. Hopefully, in several months we'll have you all back and by the end of the year we'll be able to give you your cuts back."

More drama followed when Dave had to apologize to the Sales Consultants and tell them he needed to raise the prices and inform customers the delivery time would be tripled. No specials, no liners, no covers. He told them that he thought they could save the company if they all pulled together.

"The Consultants came through like the champions that they were. The remaining employees did too and before the end of the year, everyone had his or her job back."

How in the world did Dave motivate 5,000 people to hang in there?

"I believe it was trust," Dave answered. "The employees knew I never lied to them. The Sales Directors of our Consultants had trust in me. They went back to the Regional Advisors and Branch Advisors and said, 'Hang in there. Dave has never let us down before and he won't let us down this time.' We did it. Not me, *We*!"

THE PRESENT

LONGABERGER CONTINUES . . .

Of course, the Longaberger story doesn't end with yesterday. It continues to be written today.

Dave Longaberger is the Chief Executive Officer and Chairman of the Board. Tami Longaberger is President. Rachel Longaberger Schmidt is the Chief Operating Officer. Bonnie is the patron saint, shining brightly at the Basket Bees.

The employee count has grown to more than 4,500. The Consultant count has grown to over 21,000. Thousands of Longaberger Pottery products and millions of Longaberger Baskets are sold each year, generating hundreds of millions of dollars. The product line has diversified to include pottery, WoodCrafts™ dividers and eye-pleasing fabric liners.

In this section, we'll look at what's taking place today in both the Manufacturing and Sales Divisions.

We'll not only look at what's going on, but will also try to find out some secrets for why it's working so well.

FROM TREES TO BASKETS

When you look at a Longaberger Basket, what comes to mind? You might envision a product you could run down to your local store to buy. You might visualize a few weavers sitting on a front porch weaving baskets as they wave to passing traffic. And you might imagine that when they finish a basket, they hunt around for a box and mail it to you.

Well, the feeling's the same, but the porch won't hold the basket makers anymore. The shipping system has become a little more sophisticated too, although each basket is sent out with care. As a matter of fact, part of the mystery is how can the process be so large (if they're making millions of baskets, it's large!) and yet remain so personal? Perhaps the first clue in finding the answer is to look at the process used in making the baskets.

Before you can buy a Longaberger Basket, you first need to find out *how* to buy it. As you may have learned by now, they're marketed in an unusual fashion. At least at first glance. Although they could be sold in stores, they're not. They're not sold by a mass-mailed catalog either. They can only be purchased through Sales Consultants, usually at what's known as a home show.

The reasons for this account for the consistent growth of the company. At a show, which is given in someone's home, a local Longaberger Sales Consultant brings several products to display and, in her own way, tells the Longaberger Story. She (the vast majority of the Sales Consultants are women, although several male Consultants are very successful in their Longaberger careers) also tells the history behind and current uses for many of the baskets. In other words, she's creating a feeling, an atmosphere, with these products.

It's a feeling of being back home on the farm, a feeling of old-fashioned American quality and a feeling that these baskets are durable products that are useful, attractive and able to be passed from one generation to the next.

As Ohio Consultant Jan Brunstetter said, "You're not just telling the story of how a quality basket is made, but you're also establishing that emotion that goes along with the basket."

Consumers can't receive that message by picking a basket off a shelf in a store. Since the show is being presented by a local Consultant in the home of a local customer who has invited some of her friends over, there's also an atmosphere of friendliness and credibility.

At a home show, a Consultant demonstrates hundreds of uses for Longaberger products. Plus, as the baskets are passed from guest to guest, they can feel the quality history and heritage in each of the baskets.

> **"YOU'RE NOT JUST TELLING THE STORY OF HOW A QUALITY BASKET IS MADE, BUT YOU'RE ALSO ESTABLISHING THAT EMOTION THAT GOES ALONG WITH THE BASKET."**
>
> **JAN BRUNSTETTER**

When you're in your friend's home (and let's face it, if she wasn't your friend you wouldn't agree to come look at the products!), you are much more receptive to the quality, beauty and utility of the products. This is increased by the fact that although you can see the products, you can't buy them on the spot. The idea is that you pay for a hand-crafted Longaberger Basket, made the same way that Dave's father and grandfather made them. So, although your money is requested at the time of the basket show, you won't receive your handmade basket for another few weeks.

LONGABERGER PURCHASES MAPLE LOGS ONLY FROM FORESTERS WHO PRACTICE SELECTIVE HARVESTING METHODS.

When your Consultant sends your order in, the next stop is at The Longaberger Company in Dresden, Ohio. Now the basket making process begins. And as was mentioned earlier, although the weavers would probably be able to work on a porch as some might envision, it would have to be a porch the size of a few football fields to accommodate the thousands of weavers and manufacturing employees.

The basket making process begins with trees! That's right, the Longaberger facility in Hartville receives actual trees from forests in Ohio, West Virginia, Pennsylvania, Michigan and New York. Specifically, hardwood maple for the baskets and handles. Eventually, Longaberger will even have its own logging crews to select, cut and deliver the trees. Making sure there will be an ample supply of maple trees is of paramount concern to the company, so trees are bought only from foresters who practice selective harvesting, the selection of only mature hardwood maple trees within a stand. This gives the saplings an opportunity to grow and regenerate the species. Fortunately, according to a Forest Service report, the supply of hard maple actually increases each year!

> I COULDN'T HELP BUT THINK THAT WE COULD HAVE BEEN IN A TIME WARP AROUND THE TURN OF THE CENTURY WITH J.W. LONGABERGER.

THE PROCESS FROM LOGS TO BASKETS

I assumed they would have the wood prepared for them. But I learned that Longaberger performs every step in the basket making process.

When the Grade A, ten foot long logs are delivered by long flatbed trucks, they are debarked, then cut into 42 and 62 inch lengths. Next, they are immersed in 200-256 degree steam vats for 14 to 18 hours, depending on the logs' thickness and the season of the year. The steam causes the wood to be more flexible or pliable. As a matter of fact, the workers measure each log to ensure a moisture count of at least 40% at veneering time and 20% at weaving time.

MAPLE LOGS ARE LOADED INTO A SPECIAL ROOM WHERE THEY'RE "COOKED," MAKING THEM MORE PLIABLE.

After a brief cooling period, the "cooked" logs are placed on a lathe which rotates them at a high rate of speed. Razor sharp blades are lowered on the spinning logs, much the same way you'd peel a potato or apple.

As thin veneer sheets are created, a worker on each side pulls the strip out about 15 feet and then tears the sheet off and pulls another veneer sheet out. Each sheet is graded for quality. Rejected sheets are manually pushed into a huge century-old furnace. The furnace was the only thing that was salvaged from the earlier factory fire.

The furnace is used to heat the factory and cook the logs. I might add that on the particular February morning that I visited, it felt good to stand close to it and watch the lathe and the workers in action. It was a very "homey" atmosphere with the furnace blazing and the workers taking such pride and pleasure in their work. I couldn't help but think that with the exception of a new lathe, we could have been in a time warp around the turn of the century with Daddy John Longaberger.

MAPLE LOG BLOCKS BECOME VENEER ON ONE OF THE LATHES AT PLANT TWO IN HARTVILLE.

As Lola Eddy, former Hartville Plant Manager and the first person ever to retire from Longaberger, said, "We have good quality and good workers. I think they feel at home here. We are proud of our work, our people and Dave."

The trees are bought in their prime, which costs extra. Even so, only 40% of the maple is chosen as acceptable for baskets and handles. The standards for quality are an absolute priority, free of knots or other imperfections.

The sheets are then cut to various widths called strips or splints. The splints are hand sorted for quality and measured for exact thickness, and stored in refrigerated rooms to keep them flexible and fresh. Even then, their usability is limited to only a very few weeks.

Hartville is also responsible for dyeing the splints that will be woven into some of the basket styles. Walking into the dyeing room is like walking inside a rainbow! During our visit, the workers were busy dyeing the splints for Easter baskets. The floor, the tables, everywhere we looked, splints were spread out in bouquets of color. The Longaberger Manufacturing Division has developed its own process for dyeing the splints. The popularity of colored decorative splints has caused this division to grow tremendously.

At this point, most of the splints and handles are shipped 100 miles south to the Manufacturing Campus just outside of Dresden. Some baskets are also made in Hartville.

In Building A on the Manufacturing Campus, the splints are distributed to the weavers. Each weaver has a station which includes a vertical pole with a form for the basket. This is called a "horse." A form is a wooden mold around which the weavers construct the basket. All horses and forms are made the same way J.W. Longaberger made them. "We used to put a rope around a horse and lay corn on the floor for it," Dave remembered with a laugh.

The weavers stand (not sit) by their baskets, pushing, pulling and hugging the basket. That's why each basket is said to be made with tender loving care!

COLORED SPLINTS DECORATE MANY LONGABERGER BASKETS.

THESE LOGS WILL SOON BE ON THEIR WAY TO BECOMING FAMOUS LONGABERGER BASKETS.

The first step in creating a basket is to make the bottom. Bottoms are made by forming specialists for most baskets. Instead of weaving baskets, they create the basket bottom. Next, a weaver takes the basket bottom and places it on the horse and bends the splints around the mold. The weaver then adeptly weaves in and out of the vertical splints to form the basket.

After every three or four rows of weaving, the weaver will take a tapper and tap down the weaves, ensuring a tightly woven, and strong basket.

This process must be learned perfectly for the basket to have the proper symmetry and durability. Spaces between the weaves must be the same and corners have to be tight.

CREATING A BASKET BOTTOM.

A BASKET MAKING TEAM MEMBER ADDS THE LONGABERGER LOGO SPLINT TO A BASKET BOTTOM.

Upon completion of weaving to the desired height, the weaver trims the vertical splints (called a haircut) and tacks a band at the top. Basket collectors informed me that the tiny cracks that are created from the tacks for the band and copper rivets for the handles are very important.

I think it's worth mentioning that at this point, the weaver thinks of the basket as his or hers. Dave Longaberger gave those instructions back when the first baskets were being made, "Make the basket like you were making it for yourself."

A BASKETMAKER POSITIONS THE BASKET BOTTOM ON A FORM, WHICH IS ATTACHED TO A WEAVING HORSE.

THE BASKET BEGINS TO TAKE SHAPE.

Since every part of the baskets is handmade, no two baskets are quite the same. After all, each basket is made on a different form, by different weavers, bottom makers and others you'll soon read about. When you get right down to it, no two baskets are alike because no two weavers or trees are alike! And that's part of the baskets' appeal – each basket is different.

However, these baskets are amazingly similar to the baskets J.W. Longaberger made. They're made from the same forms, the same forests, using the same techniques.

The weavers are paid on a "piecemeal" basis and enjoy their work, but realize the more they do, the more they earn. Experienced, skilled weavers have the opportunity to make over $40,000.

The manufacturing building is an impressive sight with hundreds of weavers simultaneously making baskets. The dress is casual, the pace is fast. The weavers are young and old, male and female, hometown natives and transplants. Music videos and company updates are shown on dozens of televisions placed throughout the production area. L-TV, or Longaberger Television, is an in-house studio, and fills the air along with employees' conversation and the tap-tapping of tacks into the baskets. Couriers hurry more supplies and finished baskets back and forth.

Building A is over a quarter of a million square feet in size. You could put seven buildings the size of the old plant in this one. It was built by Longaberger Construction. It's also fully heated and air conditioned.

THE BASKETMAKING FLOOR

The weaver's final duty is something that has become very special to a Longaberger Basket owner: signing and dating the basket. Turn any Longaberger Basket over and you'll find the weaver's initials with a date under them. The message: This isn't just a basket, it's a Longaberger Basket.

**A LONGABERGER TRADITION —
THE WEAVER'S INITIALS AND DATE.**

**EACH BASKET IS CAREFULLY INSPECTED
TO ENSURE ITS QUALITY.**

The baskets are examined for quality. Very few baskets are rejected. The reason is simple, the workers do it right the first time. This has been especially true since the re-introduction of basket-making teams. In a team, the entire basket is made by a group, working together. That way, any potential problems can be solved on the spot.

**THE MESSAGE:
THIS ISN'T JUST A BASKET, IT'S A
LONGABERGER BASKET.**

LEATHER HINGES ARE ATTACHED TO A BASKET.

This is a stark contrast to several studies in the '80s which showed that almost 25% of American factories' work forces were dedicated to fixing rejected or faulty parts. Longaberger employees work hard on the basket once, which prevents that second or third go around. It's one of the reasons they flourished when other factories faded.

A craftsperson then puts a lid on the baskets, if needed. The lids are attached with leather hinges instead of metal ones. These have proven to be more durable and aesthetic. Each lid has to be fitted to its basket since dimensions vary slightly.

The handles are then formed by placing them in 100 degree water for 20 minutes and curving them around a form, the same way J.W. Longaberger did it. The handles are attached with tacks for stationary handles and rivets for swinging handles.

HANDLES ARE PLACED IN A FORM AFTER BEING SUBMERGED IN VERY HOT WATER.

At this point, many of the baskets are stained. The basket is then packed and placed on the delivery truck en route to your home.

HANDLES ARE ATTACHED BY HAND.

BASKETS ARE CAREFULLY PACKAGED.

POTTERY AND BASKETS REUNITED

A major development at Longaberger in the early '90s was the introduction of a line of pottery. It was only a matter of time before baskets and pottery would be reunited.

History of Pottery

While J.W. Longaberger bent over his weaving horse working wet strips of maple into baskets, craftsmen in nearby towns bent over potters wheels, spinning clay into another kind of handmade masterpiece - pottery.

Known as the "Pottery Capital of the World," eastern Ohio towns produced the world's finest china from their abundant earthen veins of natural clay.

Potters and basket makers both took natural materials, wood and clay, and crafted them into sturdy, beautiful household products. But there's even more of a connection between potters and J.W. Longaberger, one which his son Dave would never forget.

Longaberger Pottery is created by artisans in East Liverpool, Ohio.

WOVEN TRADITIONS™ POTTERY.

Most of J.W.'s business consisted of making large, round, steel strip-reinforced pottery ware baskets. These baskets were used by potters to transport unfinished pottery during the pottery-making process. They served the function held largely by boxes today. J.W. sold a dozen of these baskets for $12.50 to potters across the state.

In 1990, the Longaberger Company decided to renew the traditional connection between pottery and baskets. The exclusive Woven Traditions™, a line of Longaberger Pottery®, was introduced. Each year new pieces are added.

Longaberger Pottery receives a light coating of lead-free glaze before being fired at 2,000 degrees for up to 12 hours. This unique firing temperature, in addition to the exclusive clay body recipe, results in highly functional, versatile pottery that withstands great variation in temperature.

Longaberger Pottery is a brand name of china made for us in the renown pottery town of East Liverpool, Ohio. It includes dinnerware and accessories. The pottery has high industry standards for strength, chip resistance, impact resistance and thermal shock resistance. The pottery's glazed foot allows the customer to stack the dinnerware without fear of scratching. The dinnerware can be taken from a casual to formal setting easily with a simple change of surroundings (tablecloth, napkins, etc.).

Tradition is the key word for Longaberger Pottery. Both the baskets and pottery are produced in remarkably large numbers by the same processes used in the early 1900s. The connection between J.W. and pottery had to be restored, in Dave, Tami and Rachel's minds, to renew another of the true arts for Longaberger customers.

The pottery is beautiful. We have several pieces in our kitchen and enjoy using them for many purposes. As a matter of fact, my wife Andrea once filled our small (pottery) pitcher with flowers for a centerpiece at a birthday party for her mother. Her mother asked why she didn't give her the pitcher for a present!

How do Longaberger Consultants feel about the pottery?

"I'll admit, when I first heard about pottery, I was a bit skeptical," said Lori Hoipkemeier, Regional Advisor, from Burke, Virginia. "But, when I saw its unique design and heard the connection and close history between pottery and baskets, I quickly changed my mind."

"I'm really excited about the Longaberger Pottery," offered Kay Cox, Regional Advisor, from Greenwood, Indiana. "It's functional, decorative and collectible. These pieces are an excellent enhancement to the baskets."

"I've always carried a few pieces of pottery to incorporate into my basket display at shows," responded LuAnn Kuyper, Sales Director, from Urbandale, Iowa. "The fresh, clean look is fabulous and the design is simple, yet elegant, and best of all, it's not limiting to any one decor."

Alice Hanley, a Regional Advisor from the rural area of Clear Lake, Iowa, has been with Longaberger for less than ten years. "The pottery can be compared to basket sales from a few years ago. They were relatively new and had to be tested. Now basket sales are great. When the pottery first came out, my customers had to test it. But once they began to use it in their homes, they had to have more. Also, I use it every day and I can tell about how my family, which includes three children, uses it. Therefore, in a time when money is tight, I can offer a quality product that will last. I love it and it shows. My customers trust my opinion. The customers who experimented by buying one dinner set are now buying the entire set. They value quality."

Barb Scholten, a Regional Advisor from Granville, Ohio, recalls, "The first thing that impressed me about the pottery was using it three times a day with my very small children. Once I started using it, I realized it really was what Longaberger said it was - durable and beautiful. So, I felt good about telling customers it was not only attractive, but 'tough stuff.' In the years we've had it, I've never chipped a piece. That opens customers' eyes. They like the idea of durability and they love the Woven Traditions pattern. Another thing that I love about the pottery is that it adds a whole new dimension to the shows and created a new clientele which is interested in pottery.

"The very first week that Longaberger began selling dinnerware, I didn't know a whole lot to say about it. I had it sitting out, and briefly mentioned that we'd just added it. A customer said, 'This is everything I have been looking for in dinnerware for my family (including five children).' She bought 12 place settings and has continued to add pieces as they become available. She has yet to chip a piece."

LONGABERGER — LEADERSHIP

When you enter the Manufacturing Building where hundreds of basketmakers are crafting the wooden splints into baskets, you can feel it. It's a relaxed but energy-charged atmosphere. It's a productive but enjoyable setting. It's music in the air, smiles on faces, talk, laughter and a great deal of pride. It's exciting!

These workers are proud of their baskets.

They're proud that they make the best baskets in the world.

They're proud that these baskets have become collector's items, to be passed from one generation to another.

They're proud of the Longaberger reputation.

They're proud of a tradition that they're continuing 100 years down the road from Daddy John Longaberger and the Dresden Basket Factory.

They're proud of their company's growth.

They're proud of The Longaberger Company.

As we interviewed employees, Consultants, customers and even Dresden citizens, we asked them why they felt the way they did about The Longaberger Company. We kept hearing "trust."

These people trust Dave. They believe that he has their best interest at heart always. They believe in his honesty. They like his straightforward and humble manner. They also feel that he believes in them.

"Dave believed in us," long-time employee Judy McGee said. "If you've got somebody behind you saying you can do it, then you're going to prove you can."

That seems to be a very important trait of the successful companies in the last part of this century – trust. Management trusts employees. Employees trust management.

TAMI AND RACHEL

Charleen Cuckovich, Sales Director, added, "Trust is a very important word to our Consultant business. For example, a few years ago, during our financial crisis, we had a six, eight and even a 12-month delivery delay on a particular hamper.

"But they got every order out. Dave told the Consultants that they would get their baskets. It would take a long time, but they would get them. They knew then that they would because Dave is a man of his word. That's very important to Consultants hundreds and thousands of miles away. He's never lied to me. That's the difference between trusting and not trusting."

> **THEY'RE PROUD OF A TRADITION THAT THEY'RE CONTINUING 100 YEARS DOWN THE ROAD FROM DADDY JOHN LONGABERGER AND THE DRESDEN BASKET FACTORY.**

I found it interesting that even though Dave has had to make unpopular decisions, the employees and Consultants still believe in him. He interacts with the employees constantly. He doesn't want to be called *Mr. Longaberger.* He just wants to be called "Dave" or "Popeye." He has no assigned parking space. He drives a Jeep. He encourages employees to candidly tell him their problems. On more than one occasion, Dave has surprised Longaberger's management team by telling the employees and Consultants exactly what was going on in the company. That's why they trust him.

"That's right," says Sales Director Jean Rinehart. "Dave's continuing presence, his sharing with others, his humor and his honesty cause us to continue to believe in him."

LONGABERGER MANAGEMENT STYLE

Dave Longaberger turned a one person business into a combined operation of over 25,000 people that's growing significantly each year. During its young history, the company has faced major setbacks in which Dave had to ask concessions from his employees and Sales Consultants.

These sacrifices have paid big dividends.

Rachel Longaberger Schmidt is now Chief Operating Officer of Manufacturing and Human Resources. Through a variety of innovative, people-oriented management techniques, Rachel and her management team combine the goals of increased productivity and an employee-centered small company feeling.

The message to Longaberger employees is that they're family. "If they get tired of weaving, we'll do everything we can to move them to another department," Dave said. "You see, you can talk all you want to about great management and organizational systems, but the first thing I would ask is how do your people feel about *you*?

"Quality and service are easy after you establish the answer to that question. You need your employees and they need you and you should like each other a lot. It goes back to one of my strongest beliefs. You can't be in business just for the money. At least, not if you want to be a good leader.

"They say anything that doesn't break you makes you stronger. Don't be afraid to show your weaknesses. Don't be afraid to admit you goofed. You'll be surprised at how forgiving and supportive your people will be."

"We're not perfect and we don't know everything," Rachel agreed. "So, we're looking for employee ideas, and employees like this strategy. We have to look at our own situation and what's good for the employee and what's good for the company. Theory is the vision, but there's also reality. People want to be connected and want to feel needed and part of a family."

DAVE LONGABERGER

I'm now going to try to do what others have only thought about doing – and cried hysterically at the very thought – define Dave Longaberger. Alright, I admit that might be too ambitious, so let me give a short profile of Dave. It's not intended to be all-inclusive or defining, but it may prove interesting.

Dave Longaberger is one of the most remarkable people I've ever met. He's also one of the craziest. At least I think he's crazy. But come to think of it, that's what makes him one of the most remarkable.

For example, Dave has conducted business most of his life on a handshake. He believes people when they make a promise. He assumes that others are as truthful as he tries to be. And yes, he's been burned a few times. But he persists in this belief.

Sales Director Jean Rinehart asked her Associates to describe Dave Longaberger in a word. Here are some of their repeated responses: *honest, independent, dreamer, approachable, charismatic, different* and *sincere*.

He refuses to have a savings account. "I will never, ever have a savings account. I'm afraid that if I had a savings account and I was secure, I may not work as hard. As long as I have no savings account, I will work ten times harder to make sure nothing happens to this company."

> DAVE LONGABERGER IS ONE OF THE MOST REMARKABLE PEOPLE I'VE EVER MET. HE'S ALSO ONE OF THE CRAZIEST. AT LEAST I THINK HE'S CRAZY. BUT COME TO THINK OF IT, THAT'S WHAT MAKES HIM ONE OF THE MOST REMARKABLE.

Crazy? Probably. Because he has commitment and integrity to others. I think everyone around him experiences that in a special way.

He moved out of his mansion on a hill overlooking Dresden into a more basic log cabin on a farm. He shares his farm with his horses and his three-legged dog. His lifestyle exemplifies the simple life. He could easily be on the cover of *L.L. Bean*.

Dave shuns the higher priced cars and prefers a four door Jeep. He also prefers sweaters and green work clothes (affectionately called "greenies") to business suits.

He's not happy in the office long. "Sometimes he's like a caged animal and drives us crazy, because he's happier in the manufacturing facilities or a construction worksite," Tami said. But if you catch him in the office, you'll see photos of his family, a painting of an American Indian (his favorite book is *Touch The Earth* – a self-portrait of Indian existence) and a copy of Frank Sinatra's *My Way* on the wall.

He loves to work hard and loves to laugh and believes you can do both. "I'd say 75% – 25% is a good ratio. I can only be serious for so long." For example, take the time Dave told employees that an employee dinner was going to be "very lavish." They came attired in suits and dresses. He showed up in his greenies.

Dave is known for many things. One of them happens at formal occasions, such as banquets or corporate dinners. "If I get bored, I pick up a roll and throw it," he explains. It's become a bit of a trademark. Things culminated at the Masters Appreciation Banquet, a recognition dinner for Longaberger's most senior employees. It was Dave's turn to speak. "As I walked up on stage, someone threw a roll at me. I picked it up and threw it back. Then the fight was on. Rolls were flying everywhere." The activity *Pelt Dave with dinner rolls* has become rather popular. At a recent employee recognition dinner, Dave was showered with rolls as he walked to the microphone.

"Among other things, Dad is a visionary," Tami observed. "The future keeps me excited and I think that rubs off on others," Dave agreed.

He's very interested in education because he felt that he was a victim of the system. "They found out what I didn't want to know instead of what I wanted to know. That's not helpful. I've always said if I'd had a good education, I'd be dangerous!

"But I think my greatest talent is that I like people and they like me."

THE PAST AND THE PRESENT MEET

We sat in Sandy Fannin's small cozy office and watched the snow fall. Sandy and Judy McGee have been with The Longaberger Company from its inception. They started as weavers and worked for two months before receiving their first paycheck! When I asked why she would work for nothing for two months, Sandy sighed and said, "It was Dave. He had a dream and we got involved. We thought he was crazy so we stuck around to help the poor guy out!" The company finally got on its feet and Dave paid them for all their previous work. But, at one point when things got rough again, they offered to give their paychecks back!

Those early days when Sandy and Judy were busy weaving baskets, Dave said, "One day we'll have thousands of employees and millions of dollars." They laughed, "We were sure he'd gone off the deep end then." But now they laugh at how they laughed. Dave has credibility with his employees.

"If he says, 'We're going to build a larger company,' then we know he will," Judy said. Today when Dave talks about the future, everybody listens. And if the new employees have a hard time believing what they're hearing, then the "old timers" are there to tell a story or two of how he's always achieved the goals that he's set.

A Family Spirit For Thousands

Although the numbers have changed, the feeling's the same for Longaberger employees and Consultants. At least, that's the goal. As Dave recently wrote, "Don't worry, just because we've grown doesn't mean we've lost the sense of family and tradition." And *they* have grown since the time of four weavers in a room with no heating or plumbing. But, how can you keep a family feeling with tens of thousands in the family?

Linda Rodgers, a Sales Director from Geneseo, Illinois, shared these letters to help explain how The Longaberger Company promotes a family feeling. As Linda explains, "I share this story at my shows as a means of giving my customers a glimpse of the caring attitude of Longaberger. Dave is the reason so many people are loyal to The Longaberger Company. He represents honesty and integrity . . . the very things he wanted to reinforce in my son."

> *Dear Mr. Longaberger,*
>
> *It was a really windy day today. I had to burn the trash. Mom told me to burn it. She had a bag of trash and a basket of trash for me to burn. I put the trash from the basket in first. Then I put the basket by the barrel after I put in the trash. Then I lit the fire and put in the bag. The wind blew the bag in the basket and the basket caught on fire some. I would be grateful if you could find a good weaver and see if you could repare (sic) it. Thank you very much.*
>
> *Yours truly,*
>
> *Jon Rodgers*
>
> *P.S. We're sending the wastebasket with the burn to the plant where they fix baskets. And let me know what the cost is soon. My mom sells baskets. Her name is Linda Rodgers.*

Jon received this letter a few days later:

Dear Jon,

Thank you so much for your letter of February 24th. I was sorry to read of your unfortunate experience with the basket that caught on fire, next to your trash barrel. I wanted to let you know that we received the basket for repairs.

I was impressed with the honesty you displayed in writing to me. I think you are truly an outstanding young man and that your honesty should not go unrewarded. I asked our Plant Manager to have one of our best weavers make a brand new basket for you. The new basket will be shipped to you soon, at no charge.

I do have one favor to ask of you. Could we have your permission to keep the scorched basket to display along with your letter at the Basket Bee? I would love for our visitors at the Bee to know of your honesty and integrity.

Best Regards,

Dave Longaberger

"There's a genuine love here among us all," Tami observed. "It's in the Corporate Office, the Manufacturing Campus and the Sales field. The love at Longaberger is still abounding."

"Even though the Consultants are scattered, they are made to feel like family," Charleen Cuckovich later added. "Dave, Tami and Rachel mingle with them during the (Basket) Bees. They walk the streets of Dresden in their shorts and have fun and develop a spirit of comraderie."

"We are a family. This is Dad's life. This is my life. We are the Longaberger Family," Tami said.

LEADERSHIP, LAUGHTER AND LONGABERGER

How many Chief Executive Officers of large companies can walk through their building and have someone say, "Hey, come here, I've got a joke for you," or go up to an employee and say, "Did you hear the one about . . .?"

A few years ago, Longaberger employees got together and made a contribution to the American Cancer Society. The donation included a trip to jail for the person of their choice! Guess who they picked?

The sheriff deputies marched in, picked Dave up and took him to jail. The employees loved it when the sheriff read Dave his rights.

The charge was "for being the ugliest grandfather in the county and inciting a riot in your own company." The fine was $1,000. As they were laughing and applauding Dave on his way out the door, handcuffed to his escort, he said, "I'll get you, each and every one of you." Everyone thought that was hilarious. After all, what could he do to all of them?

About an hour and a half later they found out. They heard several sirens. Several buses, escorted by police cars, surrounded the building. Dave had made a contribution to the Cancer Society for each employee to be arrested.

"I called the office," Dave remembered. "I told them to find some buses and send them to the plant. They said, 'Do you realize how much that will cost?' I said I didn't care. It was worth it."

Dave has used humor in a variety of stressful situations. It's been found to be one of the best antidotes for corporate or personal stress. He's also used humor just to pass the time. Take for example the time he owned a grocery store.

A teenage boy asked Dave to put his soft drink in a bag. Dave said, "Sure," and opened the drink, poured it into the sack and handed it to the surprised youth. "He just stood there, holding it and staring at me and said, 'Dave, you're so stupid,' and walked out with the bag dripping on him the whole way. I think I gave him another one. He loved it."

THE FRAZEYSBURG CAPER

One day Dave asked a new employee where she was from. "Frazeysburg," she said.

"I'd rather be dead than be from Frazeysburg," Dave joked, then turned to Judy McGee, Mary Farmer and some others and said, "How many times have I told you not to hire any more people from Frazeysburg?" At the time, Dave was wearing his greenies and boots and had not bothered to introduce himself.

Suddenly, the unsuspecting new employee rose to her full height and said, "And just who do you think you are?"

"I'm Dave Longaberger."

"Yeah, sure you are." ("At this point the other ladies are dying," Dave explained, "because they knew that I didn't want them to say who I was.")

"And when I first saw you I didn't like your nose," Dave said.

"Oh yeah?" she replied, "Well, I don't know if I even want to be around this company if they let jerks like you work for it. Why don't you go back outside?"

Dave just laughed and said, "Okay," and walked back outside.

A few days later, the employees came in for a meeting with Dave, including this new employee. He walked in with a suit and tie on. She turned white as a sheet. "Then her face turned 16 different colors," Dave laughed. After the meeting, she rushed up and began to apologize profusely. He just laughed and gave her a hug.

"You must have humor," Dave repeats. "Through all of our troubling times, we continued to laugh at ourselves. With a sense of humor, troubling times are not as troubled. If you lose your sense of humor, you're going to lose.

"I love to make a game out of business and that's just what it is, a game. Don't get too serious about it. If you get too serious, it can consume you. Enjoy it every day."

The torch is gradually being passed to the next generation of Longabergers. Of course, Dave is king of the company for life, but readily admits that he has two excellent leaders who are ready and able to take the company into the future. And two leaders who are capable of giving Dave the surprise of his life . . .

"IF YOU LOSE YOUR SENSE OF HUMOR, YOU'RE GOING TO LOSE."

DAVE'S GREATEST SURPRISE COURTESY OF TAMI, RACHEL AND RAQUEL

Longaberger wants its company to be a fun place to work. That's why they have parties in the plant. That's why Dave's daughters surprised him with - well, before you read who they surprised him with, you need a little background.

For years, whenever a waiter or waitress asked Dave, "Is there anything else I can get for you?" Dave would reply, "Yeah. How about Raquel Welch?"

Therefore, the Marketing Department set out to create a real surprise for Dave and fun for all. During the Basket Bee, 1991, Dave was just finishing his State of the Company speech. As he was making his way off the stage, his daughter Tami said, "Wait a minute, Dad. Come back up here. We've got a little game we want you to play."

Blindfolded, Dave subsequently played "Pick the Next Speaker," a game which was a lot of fun for the 3,000 audience members because contestants One, Two and Three were men dressed like women - husbands of some of the Sales Consultants. Dave caught on, pulled off his mask and informed Tami that he would not be choosing any of the contestants that day or *any* day.

"Okay, Dad, but you *might* be interested in Contestant Number Four. Look right over there!" And out walked Raquel Welch! Dave was dumbfounded. The crowd went wild.

Dave's first question to Raquel was, "*Are you the real one?*" His next words were, "I think I'm going to have a heart attack." Raquel subsequently made a speech and enjoyed the Bee so much that she stayed for the rest of the day.

As Rachel remembers, "I was in a meeting before the Bee when Tami brought in the purchase order for Dad to sign."

Tami said she was sorry to interrupt but she had a couple of purchase orders Dave had to sign. When Dave asked what they were for, she said that it was for the Bee. He signed them both, in a hurry to get back to the meeting.

"I scooped them up in a hurry," Tami added, "and made a quick exit. Typed on the Purchase Order was *For Raquel Welch's Services at the Basket Bee*.

"Raquel came in the night before to rehearse. Some of the Sales Consultants' husbands took Dad out to keep him out of the hotel."

"They took me all over Columbus that night," Dave said.

"So they took me to German Village and on a tour of Ohio State University," Dave laughed. "Now when I'm asked if there's anything else a waitress can get me, I say, 'Yeah, how about Raquel Welch again.'"

TAMI LONGABERGER

As President of The Longaberger Company, Tami Longaberger makes a strong case for why a career in direct sales can meet both personal and professional goals:

"More than any other genre of business enterprise, direct selling provides opportunity for literally anyone willing to work hard to nurture their own business. More than any other single industry, direct selling offers real opportunity to women and minorities, the disabled, the young and the old. Regardless of a person's education or experience, national origin or beliefs, direct selling helps people realize the American Dream.

"Longaberger is in the right place, at the right time and we're doing the right thing. We're in the right place because in terms of what American consumers want in the 90s, the direct selling industry is precisely on target."

TAMI CONGRATULATES THE SALES FIELD
AT BEE '93 FOR ANOTHER OUTSTANDING YEAR.

Although she worked with the company during the summers of her time in college, Tami officially began her administrative career after she graduated from Ohio State University in 1984.

She married Mike Kaido in 1987 and now balances her career with raising two children, Claire and Matthew.

"For the first two years, I learned from long-time Longaberger professionals Anita Rector, Sherry Colling and Marge Shipley. The next six years I was more under Dad's wing. Beginning in 1992, I've worked with a free reign, although Dad still feels free to tell me if he disagrees!" Tami summarized.

When asked to identify milestones in her career, Tami was silent for over a minute. Then she reflected:

"In 1986, I was given the authority to change our sales policies and sales administration. The policies were adequate when we were a one million dollar company, but needed a new structure for our present size which, at the time, was a 30 million dollar company. As a matter of fact, that's still a milestone today. Our company's rapid growth necessitates a constantly changing structure. It's a good problem, but it's still a critical issue.

"I'm also proud of our team's accomplishment in 1986 for creating Longaberger's first sales campaigns which included four-color sales literature for the first time.

"I was also given the opportunity to critique and change the entire sales operation, which resulted in changes to every sales-related area from the mail room to the sales field."

Rachel offered an additional insight to Tami's impact on the company. "Look what the Sales field has achieved. Tami has helped create an environment and structure in which they can excel and enjoy the process. Her sales support and administration have allowed the Sales field to create and enjoy incredible growth."

"We have been fortunate enough to put together a Sales and Marketing team that meets the challenges of a 300 to 500 million dollar company," Tami said.

"I think it's important to point out, though, that the list of what we *need* to do is greater than the list of what we've done."

RACHEL LONGABERGER SCHMIDT

Rachel Schmidt is Longaberger's Chief Operating Officer.

"Rachel is able to get things done," Tami observed. "When you're talking about the demands of our company, that's no small task! She has been able in a very short period of time to dramatically impact employee productivity as well as their benefits."

"Rachel believes in my principles more seriously than anyone else," Dave said. "Although I've talked about them for years, she was the first to put them into action throughout manufacturing."

Rachel graduated from high school in 1985, was married in 1986 to Doug Schmidt, had her first of three children, Kaitlin, and went to work

RACHEL LONGABERGER SCHMIDT

for Longaberger at minimum wage. Dustin David was her second child, followed by Benjamin Douglas.

"I went to college for a quarter and dropped out. I didn't want to wait. I wanted to go directly into the business. I felt like a basketball player on the bench saying, "Gee, Coach, put me in!"

"One day I was thinking about who should take over Human Resources," Dave remembered. "At that exact moment, Rachel walked past my office door. I jumped up and asked her to come into my office and sit down.

"'You're going to be VP of Human Resources,' I said.

"'But, Dad, I don't know anything about it.'

"'Good!'"

"I think the fact that Rachel doesn't have a degree and programmed thinking has given her credibility with the employees," Dave said. "Instead of handing out the answers, her attitude has been one of *help me*. That's something the employees hadn't heard. She has also been able to give employees more attention than I ever did." Rachel subsequently also became responsible for Longaberger Manufacturing.

"I view Manufacturing as the defense," Rachel observed. "The Sales field promises and Manufacturing has to live up to the promise. We want to be *yes* people! We want to live up to company and customer expectations.

"We also want to make the Mission Statement, 'To Stimulate a Better Quality of Life,' come true. We want to make Longaberger the best place to work in the world!

"My goal for managing our thousands of employees is to listen and to recognize employees. Management is not perfect, so we're looking for employee ideas. Employees know what offsets quality and why. They know what needs to be changed. We value employee input.

"We listen to our team through focus groups, work teams and strong manager-employee relationships. We try to recognize through a family feeling. Everyone wants to feel connected. Through our work team philosophy, when you're absent, your team members are concerned. I'm very excited about our work team concept. We've reduced absenteeism, increased morale, reduced manufacturing steps and created well-rounded crafts artisans.

"Our quality continues to go even higher. The plant's work teams have created the spirit of cooperation to increase quality instead of a separate department acting as the basket police.

"Our work teams have enabled us to go 'back to the future,' by giving us a small company feeling again.

"I received a letter the other day that tells me we're on the right track. It said, 'Dear Rachel, When I began at Longaberger I had no money, no benefits and low self-esteem. Through the benefits, Employee Assistance Program and working environment, I now have a life. I feel good about who I am and who I'm working for. I also feel that I have a new family.'

"When Kaitlin was five, she asked, 'Mom, what do you do?' I thought about it for a minute and answered, 'I help people work better.' Live better, actually. Through all the programs, our goal is for people to *blossom*. I just help people believe in themselves. I tell employees: *Sure you can do it!* 'I can?' *Absolutely!* 'Maybe I can!' And they do, and go on to achieve more and more.

"We are continually searching for ways to recognize our employees. If it's important for Consultants in the Sales field, it's just as important for employees in Dresden. So, we have, for example, Family Day each year. This is for all Longaberger employees and their families. We provide all sorts of rides, food, everything else that goes along with a county fair, and it's all free. You can see it in the faces of the children - 'My parent is important because he/she works at Longaberger.'

"We bring nationally-known entertainers to Dresden to perform just for the employees. We have recognition dinners for employees with over five years and over ten years of service. We have fun days such as Beach Day and encourage employees to have fun and dress up on Halloween, and, wear green on St. Patrick's Day. And, of course, we provide such services as free doctors' visits, with doctors on site in our Health Clinic. We've also arranged for the prescriptions to be delivered on site. We're in the process of creating other employee services such as child care and banking."

TO DELEGATE EFFECTIVELY, YOU'VE GOT TO LET GO

"I think a lot of companies make mistakes by not letting their people go," Dave said. "Let me explain what I mean. A friend of mine told me something that I've never forgotten. She had a ten year old son die of leukemia. As the years passed, I asked how she was. She said the holidays were the hardest because they reminded her so much of him. And then she said it. 'Well, sometimes I have to let go in order to hang on.' She was trying so hard to hang on to the past until she finally decided she had to let go and begin to live again.

"I've learned that to a degree, I have to do that in business. I have to let my staff go in order to hang on to them."

Rosabeth Moss Kanter emphasized in her book, *Men and Women of the Corporation,* that the more people who have power in an organization, the stronger the organization.

"The Longaberger Company depends on good people in the plants and in the field," Charleen Cuckovich said. "As long as we continue to have that freedom, we'll flourish. I've always felt that freedom to grow and try new things with Dave."

The Longaberger Company chooses good people, tells them what it wants and lets go. The parameters are broad for creativity and productivity as long as they stay within Dave's people-person philosophy.

LONGABERGER EXCELLENCE

The Longaberger business philosophy didn't originate from a text book. It came from common sense and fairness. As the business grew, Dave kept following the golden rule with his employees.

"Although Dad didn't go to college, he's been practicing all of the principles that business just now seems to be discovering," Rachel said. "Studies now prove that people would rather have freedom, flexibility and creativity and even take a pay cut than have more money and do one specific job."

"Many of our Consultants and Advisors are very innovative and have introduced wonderful ideas about selling, decorating and even managing, which has greatly added to our success," Sales Director Joan Henning observed. "There's definitely freedom for creativity."

"When we first began," Dave explained, "there were very few basket manufacturers in the United States. Our competition was foreign and we were making a product that was labor intensive with the finest materials. The question was, could we compete? But while we're trying to compete, how do we keep our people motivated?"

It's no secret that America has lost entire industries to Japan, Korea, Taiwan and other markets. Millions of factory workers have lost their jobs due to their plants' inability to compete. How then was Longaberger able to successfully compete with these other countries?

"I've learned that people like the story of how our baskets were first made by my grandfather, then my father, now me and my daughters and one day by my grandchildren. We're not just a basket company – we're a family business. People like that. They like that personal touch. We're not just a family limited by blood either. Our Longaberger family includes our weavers, employees of all types and Consultants. Our extended family likes that. Each basket is a little different from any other basket because it's handmade by a person who signs that basket. That family spirit is marked by a high quality."

Like other successful companies throughout the world, Longaberger places a high priority on quality of materials and workmanship.

Fred Smith, Chairman and founder of the Federal Express Corporation, said, "More and more we make our own buying decisions based on quality. And so I think we can all agree, no matter what business we're in, the goal is quality and the challenge is reaching it. People come in two very important forms in any company: first and foremost are our customers and first and foremost are our employees. I'm not sure there's a second place when it comes to people. . . "

"We're constantly alert to the customer," Dave said. "We want to provide the very best customer service. I want us to be known because of the Longaberger story, our quality and our service."

Longaberger Baskets are more expensive than a basket you could buy in a department store. But they're also made to last. The handles are sturdy. The baskets are durable. The results are in, consumers are willing to pay more for quality. In the long run, it's the most economical decision because you won't need to buy a replacement basket when this one wears out. The message is simple: you pay more but you get more.

Quality has remained incredibly high with a great deal of pride of ownership by the weavers. The manufacturing defect rate is less than half of one percent and less than one percent of the *millions* of baskets purchased are returned.

Dave summed it up. "I've learned that numbers alone aren't enough. I guess I could sit here and say that we have sophisticated systems and a brilliant game plan, but that game plan is just people."

IMPROVING THE PROCESS

Exciting opportunities and innovations are taking place on the
Longaberger Manufacturing Campus.

"We are continuously looking for ways to improve the total basket
making process," said Ken Cramer, Director of Research and
Development, instrumental in implementing work teams. "We saw the
need to eliminate and collapse the number of steps it took to make a
basket. Therefore, we redesigned the manufacturing process. They are
now made by work teams, which include every stage of basket making
as before. Only now, you have a group of about 20 people working
together as a team.

"This has reduced the time it takes to make a basket. It reduced our
defects even further. It allows us to use a better product. We even include
someone from Quality Assurance as part of the team. This means a team
is able to immediately fix a basket making problem.

"The work teams also provide opportunities for cross training which
helps keep an employee's morale up. It also allows team members to
help each other out. The work teams have proven to be an exciting
innovation at Longaberger. They've opened up areas of employee
cooperation and have strengthened and renewed relationships."

Work teams have also done something else. "They've increased
morale," Rachel said. "Members of the teams feel close to each other.
The physical set up of the work team enables employees to talk to each
other while they work. This strengthens our goal for making the day fun
and enjoyable as well as productive. As a matter of fact, we even have
some husband and wife teams that work together. They love it."

Another innovation at Longaberger involves the election of
supervisors, a process in which the employees vote for such
management personnel as their work team leader. Tom Reidy, Vice
President of Legal Affairs, points out, "The elections eliminate suspicion
of favoritism."

"We've also created a Fair Treatment Process for our employees," Reidy said. "This is an effort by the corporation to resolve misunderstandings impartially. The first stage consists of assigning a mediator with counseling background to resolve the problem. Most problems are solved in this stage. Problems not solved in this phase move to the second stage, the Fair Treatment Committee, with the mediator acting as the employee's advocate. Longaberger's attitude is one of attempting to go the extra step to save jobs.

"That's why we offer employee assistance programs, personal and career counseling, a health clinic, safety and wellness programs and a wide variety of other employee benefits."

LONGABERGER LESSONS

A funny thing. As Dave was taking me from one location to another, he calmly shared a wealth of experienced-based wisdom. Not just in the Jeep, but in restaurants, in the plants and then here in Memphis (my home), too. I decided that I better start writing it down.

I've been associated with leaders of large corporations and cities, authors of business best sellers and national entertainers and celebrities. Dave Longaberger is as knowledgeable about business as anyone I've ever met. And he's able to translate that information into action. He was just making conversation, but I think it's a valuable part of the book. It helps you more fully understand his insights and tools. They're simple and effective.

I'd encourage you to recognize and utilize this practical, proven information both personally and professionally. Here are Dave's thoughts on selected subjects.

SERVICE

"Good service comes from employees having a high degree of trust and respect for management and the company. Then and only then will good service come. You don't get good service from a system; you get it from an employee."

SELF-DOUBT

"Self-doubt is very much a form of failure, but I wouldn't give a pinch of salt for anybody without self-doubt. Self-doubt can and will build strength and confidence. Even with self-doubt, you can be productive and successful. It's using a method I call LTD. Look at it, Think about it and then Do something about it.

"For example, take a business opportunity you're presented with. Look at it. Does it look good? Can you feel it? Can you feel the chemistry that you have, the gut feeling that you have? I like to relate it to the fact that not every woman is attracted to every man or every man is attracted to every woman. Look at the opportunity that comes along. Look at it from the inside out. What do you see? Get that picture painted in your mind.

"THEN, IF I DID FAIL IN MY OLDER YEARS, I COULD SIT ON THE PORCH WITH GREAT SATISFACTION IN MY HEART THINKING TO MYSELF, WELL I TRIED. AT LEAST I WON'T BE SITTING THERE IN THE CHAIR THINKING I WISH I'D TRIED.

"Then Think about it, but don't go to anybody else! You know better than anyone else at this point. Get your thoughts together. Research answers to your questions. When you have thought about it short term and long term, go one step further and ask yourself, 'What else can this lead into?'

"Continue to think about it. Is there a market or can you create one? If it fails, what will happen at the worst and at the best? I call it your insurance policy. For example, I knew when I quit Nickles Bakery for the restaurant I could always go back to the bread route. The same with the grocery store and the same with the basket business. Develop an insurance policy. Of course, you are the policy!

"Then Do. Look, Think, Do. The greatest of intentions are of no use unless you put them into action. This is not Look, Think, *Talk* – it's *Do!* Don't talk about it, Do it!"

MISTAKES

"Fifty years of mistakes, that's me. But I learned from them. Not just then, but I'm still learning from those mistakes. I love to make mistakes! I learn much more from mistakes than I ever learned from my successes. I believe you achieve through 15% Intelligence, 35% Common Sense and 50% Mistakes. Failures are not final. They're the beginning. You must fail before you can succeed.

"If I have to make ten decisions today, I know beyond a shadow of a doubt that 50% of them will be wrong. Now, maybe you're smarter than that, so you won't have as many opportunities to learn."

"Dad taught us that it's okay to take risks. I've seen him fail many times," Tami said. "For example, he once bought a food truck to sell food to workers at construction sites. It didn't work out. He admitted it and moved on."

EMPLOYEE MOTIVATION

"Employee motivation is simple. First, you must believe in what you're saying and doing. You can't fool them for long. Second, you must have a proven track record. To get that, do what you say you're going to do. Third, when you're wrong, apologize. You're going to make mistakes like anyone else.

"Fourth, don't ask anyone to do what you haven't done. Fifth, don't hide from them, talk! Sixth, don't be afraid to laugh . . . a lot. Seventh, don't duck hard questions. Tell them what they want to hear and show them what they want to see. Eighth, show strength, firmness and fairness."

LEADERSHIP

"There's a difference between leading and driving. Perhaps you can drive cattle, but it doesn't work well on people. People always come first. Fifty percent of any business is People, 30% is the Product and 20% the Systems. Systems should not be designed to run people. People must run the systems.

"You don't need an M.B.A. to be a good leader. Just use common sense. I think leadership comes down to three words: Comfort, Trust and Humor."

HUMOR

"Humor is a state of mind. I believe it is very healthy to mix business with humor. Seventy-five percent of the day should be spent in work, mixed with 25% humor. Humor is the best relaxer. Humor is the best motivator. You don't have to grit your teeth to be successful. If you can't relax and enjoy it, it's not worth it. Laugh and live. If you're not laughing, you're not living. Or at least you won't be very long."

"Humor is very important to the Longaberger Company and the Longaberger family," Rachel observed. "Dad, Tami and I will be very intense and in a heated argument. The room is tense. Then someone will make us laugh and it takes the pressure off."

"I got my sense of humor from my mother," Dave said. "She imparted the gift of humor to all of her children. My brother Gary is one of the funniest people I've ever met."

REST

"There is not enough said about rest. The person who works from daylight to dusk gets tired and older. I try to stop work at five o'clock. It gives me time for myself and relaxation.

"If you work hard during the day, you'll get enough done. Rest is as needed as work. I think that fact is easy to overlook. It's needed for your energy level and your attitude."

COMMON SENSE

"Somebody told me if schools could teach common sense, we'd have more successful businesses. Well, they can and you can teach yourself. Somehow we've been conditioned to believe we shouldn't trust our better judgment, our instincts. We've left things in the hands of the experts and now the experts are going full circle to teach us how to use sound, practical judgment."

QUALITY

"In whatever you do, quality gets the higher price. It's true in the grocery business; it's true in the delivery business; it's true in the computer business; it's true in the basket business. I learned back in the restaurant business that even though my prices were 25% higher than the others, I still had the largest customer share. The reason was that I listened to Bud and Florence Hall, proud owners of Hall's Brown Cow restaurant in Zanesville, Ohio, who advised, 'Dave, if you give them good quality and good service, you'll have no problem.'

"Quality must be the heart and soul of all employees and the sales field. Quality comes from people with pride and respect for their company and what it does and who they are. Then, you'll always have good quality. Quality is simply doing it right the first time.

"Finally, you must sell your quality not just in price and not just in service, but it trickles down into your personality, into your attitude, into your humor, into you! You have to be that committed to quality and it will be there, I guarantee it."

MANAGING

"We let our employees evaluate our supervisors, not the supervisors evaluate the employees. The only people who truly know how well the supervisors are doing are the people working under them. We try to train the supervisors from feedback in employee evaluations.

"The bottom line in management is employee trust. Simple as that. If a manager or supervisor doesn't have that trust, you'd better reposition him or her quickly.

"You have to show that you can be trusted. This is true whether you're managing a business, a family, an opportunity or a personal life.

"Managing is like the four seasons. In the summer, the flowers are out and the business is good. But as the fall approaches, Mother Nature is giving you signs that you better store some food for the winter. So you become more cautious. You must be able to read fall signs that things are going to get worse before they get better. From a manager's point of view, you not only have to see it, but effectively and sympathetically communicate it to your employees.

"Then comes winter and it gets worse. Relationships may deteriorate. Fingers may be pointed and there seems to be no relief in sight. But around here, the ice on the river begins to thaw. That's the sign. It never fails. Spring comes and brings with it new hope, new energy, new satisfaction, new projects and new flowers. A good manager has to be able to manage in all types of seasons."

COMPETITION

"Don't be afraid of competition! It's your best source of information. Use LTD. Look at your competition. Think about their strengths and weaknesses and then Do. Competition is the best source of information and it's free.

"I realize that competition can be very rough. But it's a reality and you have to make it a learning ground instead of a permanent roadblock. I think competition ultimately makes you better. It's exciting!"

SELLING

"Selling anything is simply selling yourself. If you can't do that, you won't sell your product or service successfully. Be yourself. Don't copy someone else's style."

CRISIS

"I guess we all have some type of business or personal crisis on a weekly basis. It could be financial, organizational, over commitment, unhappy customers, problems with a vendor, the commode won't flush or the TV is on the blink. There's no way to avoid them. I think the way you deal with them measures your success as a person.

"For some, change is a crisis. Well, don't let it be, because it will happen with or without you. And it's much more enjoyable if it happens with you. Nothing remains the same. It's easy to want things to remain the same, but you have to be adaptable to change to survive crisis.

"I've been through a number of crises and I've always been made stronger by them. I'm more convinced than ever that you have to have at least the three tools we used to manage through crisis. You must Trust each other. You must find Comfort in each other. You must have a sense of Humor.

"Remember, crisis is not all bad. It's usually a 50-50 proposition and only you can improve the odds."

LIVING THE DREAM

"It's a crying shame that most of us are between 35 and 50 before we discover what we really like to do. The major reason I see for this is that so many people spend too much time worrying about what somebody else's opinion is. I think everyone has God given talents. You must constantly be searching for them. Feel free to dream. Think about what you enjoy doing and think about how your talents can help you reach that dream. That's what I did. I'm still doing it."

HANDICAPS

"Most handicaps are not permanent road blocks. If the fifth oldest boy of 12 children who flunked three times in elementary school, who stuttered so badly that people could barely understand him, who couldn't secure a loan from the bank to save his life, can reach his goals, so can you! Regardless of your circumstances, background or abilities, you can be successful, if you are willing to do what it takes."

Success

"Success is not measured by money, but by self-respect, satisfaction, recognition, concern for others and continual growth."

LONGABERGER MANAGEMENT PRINCIPLES

Longaberger's unique Principles of Management have gained a great deal of attention. They apply to Sales Directors, Regional Advisors and Branch Advisors. They also apply to corporations, school systems and small business. Here, in expanded form, are Dave's Management Principles, written in his unique style. They've been called exciting, refreshing, controversial, different, practical, crazy and common sense. Whatever your label for them, they seem to work.

THE 1ST PRINCIPLE, P.C.T. —
PERSONAL – CREATIVE – TECHNICAL

"Know your **PERSONAL** skills…

Understand your **CREATIVE** skills…

TECHNICAL skills come only from experience."

Personal Skills– You either have them or you don't. That does not mean, with some practice, you can't get some.

Skill means your ability to use your knowledge. But we must understand from the get go, knowledge only comes from experience. It is not how many degrees you have from a university, but how many degrees you have from life's experience.

You've heard of extrovert, introvert, left and right brain, but personal skills boil down to your character, your conduct, your reputation, your morals, your quality, your disposition, your common sense, your understanding, your enthusiasm, your good humor and your concern for what others think.

It's as simple as that and don't let anybody tell you any different!

Work on developing and improving these traits and your personal skills will improve.

Creative Skills – Can you bring things into being? Can you organize a group and carry a project through with or without help? Are you resourceful and not easily discouraged? Can you paint a picture in your mind of how you see the end result?

Technical Skills – Special and practical knowledge and being able to use that learned knowledge.

You have been given three skills – personal, creative and technical; it's your job to find out which one you have the most of.

Let me give you a personal example. I found out very early in life that school was boring to me. However, through working after school at the corner grocery, I was able to express myself. I could experiment and watch customers' reactions. I slowly started to pick up a few personal skills that I saw worked for other people. Down through the years they became habits, and as my personal skills improved, my confidence in my creative skills rose also.

But until about 1988, when I began working on this book, I discovered that I possessed very low confidence in my skills. **Then I learned that intelligence comes from understanding and understanding comes from experience and experience is knowledge.** I had become my worst critic until I realized the value of my experience.

In our management at Longaberger, personal skills are very important. A manager needs to have the technical skills to perform a job, but he or she also needs to be likable, sympathetic and encouraging.

In any successful organization, it's not the technical skills that made it successful, but the personal skills of its leaders. If employees like a leader, they will produce. If they don't, they won't. It's that simple – no big deal.

Know what your skills are. This will help you understand what to listen for, what you can learn by listening and how you can lead those working with you.

THE 2ND PRINCIPLE, THE 3 L'S —
LISTEN – LEARN – LEAD

"If you are willing to **LISTEN** to people,

willing to **LEARN** from what you listen to;

then, and only then will you learn how

to **LEAD** them."

Listen – Can you participate in a conversation without saying a word? Can you listen to the *way* someone says something as well as the words that are used? I think that listening is the hardest thing to do.

Learn – Do you gain knowledge and understanding of a skill through (a) personal study, (b) formal instruction, (c) experience, or (d) by a combination of all three? I think it's through all three.

Lead – Can you show others the way through direction?

Employees only want to know what is going on. When you tell them, they will listen. Then *you* must listen to their response. This helps you learn their wants and needs and they will want to follow you. That will make you a leader.

One day, we were having a management meeting about some problems in the handle department. Two hours passed, no solution. I then said, "Get me three of your best handle people." When they arrived, I presented them with the problem and asked, "What do you think?" Then, those of us in management listened in amazement to these front line personnel suggest several very simple and practical solutions. Thirty minutes later, we had our problem solved.

Your people know more about your business than you do – Talk to them – Listen to them.

Not too long ago, a senior officer was telling us about a new insurance program about to be introduced. I asked, "Did you ask the managers if it does what they need?"

"No."

"Then we're not ready for this meeting. Go listen. Then redo the plan. Then we'll get back together."

Once you have shown your people that you are willing to listen and to learn from them, then you will gain their trust.

THE 3RD PRINCIPLE, T.C.H. —
TRUST – COMFORT – HUMOR

"Your success will come from

other people's **TRUST** in you.

Your **COMFORT** will be their strength,

your **HUMOR** will be their comfort."

Trust – Is what it is all about. Confidence and firm belief in another's honesty, ability and reliability.

Comfort – Comes from your ability to give strength, hope, satisfaction and state of ease.

Humor – Is the best motivator. Your ability to express what is funny. It's your mood and state of mind.

I cannot say enough about trust. Of all the 54 words in the Principles, Trust is the hub of the wheel. Trust is the grease that keeps it turning. Okay, I'll quit.

The building of your organization must be on your list of top priorities after finding your skills, (PCT). Trust is and will always be the foundation of that building – without it, the foundation will give way.

Do they (customers and employees) like to have you around? Do they talk with you about things other than business? Sometimes when I eat with employees or Consultants, I say, "Okay, tonight we're not going to talk about Longaberger. Every time you say 'basket,' you owe me a quarter."

Twenty-five percent of the day should be spent in enjoying your work. Humor is the best motivator and relaxer.

You must also show comfort through unspoken words. That can be a strong statement. Take your suit off and *relax!* What's the first thing you do after work? The suit and tie come off. I would like to know who came up with the suit. It has its place in society, but not in the workplace.

If you relax…others will.

Trust builds good relationships. Good relationships will open up doors of opportunity for you. But, by all means, don't be cosmetic.

That is the one word that has built The Longaberger Company – trust. Not technical skills, but personal skills. I've worked very hard to develop trust. I want employees, Consultants, Directors, whoever, to believe what I say every time. They may not *like* what they hear, but they believe I'm being totally honest with them.

Trust, being the most important of these abilities, can sometimes be lost through disappoint in your life or your position. When trust is gone, the only thing you can do to gain it back is to have patience.

THE 4TH PRINCIPLE, P.T.R. —
PATIENCE – TIME – RESOURCES

"There is strength through **PATIENCE**.

Leave **TIME** to think and

understand your **RESOURCES**."

Patience – Do you have the strength, despite all the opposition, to stay the course and to handle the negative remarks from family, friends or foes?

Time – Can you manage and measure the time it will take to get the job done and know when it is time to kick butts or give pats on the back?

Resources – Do you have the ability and the information to handle all the difficulties and situations that will arise?

You must have patience to set your course to make it happen (call it making your luck). Go back to the first Principle, know your Personal, Creative and Technical skills, – set your course and go for it!

Having the patience is great, but timing is more important. You must look at your mental painting and set the timer for it to happen. Knowing when it is time is very important. Seize the opportunity while it is still an opportunity. That's what we did with the baskets. That's what we did with the pottery. That's what we're doing with Dresden. That's what we'll do with Longaberger Square.

If you know your Resources, keep good relationships and get your rest, when difficult times come, you can draw on them. If time is in doubt and Patience is wearing thin, then ask yourself, "Do I know what I am doing?"

THE 5TH PRINCIPLE, THE 3 D'S —
DO – DOING – DONE

"What do you want to **DO**?

What are you **DOING**?

What have you **DONE**?"

Do means – Can you achieve what you want to?

Doing – What action are you taking?

Done – What have you completed?

There are a lot of people smarter than me. There are a lot of people with more education. There are a lot of people with more technical knowledge. When you get right down to it, I'm at the bottom of the totem pole! But one thing separates me from many of them. *I moved past asking and started doing.* I learned you make a lot of mistakes but you also have a better chance of succeeding than when you do nothing.

Knowing what you would like to do and finding a way to do it is something else. This is the time to sit back and take a long look at where you are and where you need to go.

Take a mental snapshot of where you are. Look around you; do you see opportunity? Can you make an opportunity for yourself? Can you visualize that your present job or challenge will open up opportunities in some other area later?

If you truly want to Do something with your life, you must understand that other people, at times, will have to come first. Because, without people, you can't Do anything.

THE 6TH PRINCIPLE, P.P.S. —
PEOPLE – PRODUCT – SYSTEM

"Understanding that **PEOPLE**

are united by a common culture,

producing a **PRODUCT** that is linked

by a common interest and

organized into a **SYSTEM**."

Understanding your work culture is of the utmost importance to your employees and it better be to you also. Also, without the understanding and trust of the employees, you will not move very far for very long.

Having a product or service that people can believe in goes hand in hand with trust. Too many employers believe a good system is all you need. Listen, all you need is people believing in you and your product. They will help you discover a system. Too many businesses emphasize system and structure to the exclusion of people.

You don't need outside help nearly as much as you're told. Ask your employees and friends what they think and what they feel you need. The way you see yourself is different from the way they do. *It's free.*

Listen to people and learn from them. The trust will come.

Once you know how important People, Product and System are to your success, the next step is to sell it, and yourself, to others.

THE 7TH PRINCIPLE, M.M.S. —
MARKETING – MERCHANDISING – SELLING

"**MARKETING** is simply telling a good story,

MERCHANDISING yourself in the best light

and you'll have no trouble **SELLING** yourself."

Marketing – Is creating a demand for goods or services and an act for moving your product or services to the people. Simply, tell a good story.

Merchandising – Is your appearance, your language, your character, your conduct. It's displaying yourself and your product in the best light.

Selling – *You* must believe in the value and desirability for your product before you can persuade others to.

I believe we've done this with our products. We tell a good story and believe very strongly in their beauty and quality. It's not unusual to hear a Consultant say, "I love to sell baskets because they sell themselves." Well, when you combine a strong product with a quality person who tells a good story and really believes in the product, selling becomes easy and enjoyable.

Watch how other companies and people market and merchandise. Go to school at their expense. Don't make it more difficult than it is. Study why people go to a certain restaurant or supermarket or buy a particular product.

Knowing the importance of marketing, merchandising and selling can be better understood by knowing what your labor and material cost are.

THE 8TH PRINCIPLE, L.M.C. — LABOR – MATERIAL – COST

"Know and understand your **LABOR**

and **MATERIAL COST**

and keep it there."

You must always, always be looking for a better way to do things. If you haven't been, then you had better start today. Please don't rely on other people to do it for you. You must get involved. They can maintain it for you, but you must show the way.

It is very important to know what your labor and material costs are. Whatever business you're in or want to get into, join that association. Get the experience from that association. They know better than anyone what your labor and material costs should be. Talk to them.

If you can't do that, then do some experimenting by cutting your labor and material costs. You'll gain more knowledge for another day.

The only time to raise prices is when you no longer can cut labor or material costs.

The next principle will help you understand cost a lot better. But it also contains another message to management. To do what we want to do, we must understand that intelligence is the ability to understand.

THE 9TH PRINCIPLE, I.C.M. —
INTELLIGENCE – COMMON SENSE – MISTAKES

"To do what you want to do,

    take a little bit of **INTELLIGENCE**,

       a lot of **COMMON SENSE** and a great

          amount of learning from your

            MISTAKES."

Intelligence – The ability to learn from a new situation.

Common Sense – Being able to use sound practical judgment.

Mistakes – A wrong judgment. You will make them.

Intelligence is your ability to understand what you have and what you need. Experience is the knowledge you need to do what ever you want to do. (It *really* makes me mad to see some college graduates with the technical skills, thinking the world owes them a living and they have no idea that personal skills are more important to them than technical skills).

I truly believe managing people involves some intelligence, even more common sense and a great ability to learn from your mistakes.

It took me a long time to admit to others that I could only read and write at an eighth grade level. I finally learned that common sense and experience are more important than formal education or intelligence.

We just about lost our company because of a 3,000% growth in three years. I thought it was time for me to go, so I fired myself and hired a man with a degree in Business Administration and Marketing. In just three months, the Vice Presidents and Directors came to me and said, "Dave, get him out or we all go."

The man was loaded with technical skills but no personal skills. I took a good look at myself and, through the writing of this book, I was fortunate to see myself as others saw me. I discovered that I *do* have skills – personal and creative. Again, I learned this from readers like you.

It's not how many degrees in business you have, but only the degree of experience you have in managing people. You've seen it a hundred times. This so called intelligent person comes into the company and comes up with solutions to problems you didn't have until he or she got there. *Don't let it happen!* They insult your intelligence; they think you were just born yesterday or you just fell off the turnip truck.

Give me a caring person with a little sense of humor and I have a good manager.

THE 10TH PRINCIPLE, P.P.P. —
PICTURES – PLACES – PEOPLE

"Old **PICTURES**

    with memorable **PLACES**

        is all about **PEOPLE**."

Pictures – A representation of your past.

Places – A village, city, room, a particular spot.

People – The work force, the public and/or community.

The time I spent working with Steve on the first edition of this book was pretty hard at the beginning (this was virgin country I was in), until I discovered the world of knowledge in some of the old pictures I had.

I saw people I hadn't thought about for years. I remembered statements they made to me and are very helpful to me today.

The places, combined with the people of the past, form a picture that is so strong it can only help you. I know this may sound like an unusual management principle, but it helps you remember why you think and act the way you do.

Understanding that knowledge is simply experience, if you will take the time to look at some old pictures, you will see yourself as you have never seen yourself before. Those pictures will tell you of the places you've been and of the people who gave you the experience you possess today.

Longaberger Top Ten Principles

Understanding the top ten principles can help you to work in or build a very strong organization.

Know yourself.

Listen to people.

Trust people.

Have patience.

Know what you want to do.

People are first.

Market yourself.

Know your labor and material costs.

Intelligence is only understanding.

Look at old pictures.

THE 11TH PRINCIPLE, M.O.C. —
MOTIVATE – CREATE – ORGANIZE

"If you truly understand what
MOTIVATES your people, then it will
become easy to **CREATE** and
ORGANIZE to maintain a strong
management team."

The best motivator is humor. From our large annual meeting, the Bee, to a small department meeting, I try to use humor. I also think people are motivated when they feel a sense of freedom, see that their input is valued, and hear you ask them what they want and need.

I find it amazing that business is seldom positioned as fun. It's been positioned as stiff shirts and power ties and you do it because it's a living. It can also be a lot of fun.

Motivation can also come by way of incentives. I have become a big believer in them. When I began putting some incentives in place, determined by how much work was accomplished, production went up and absenteeism reduced. Let me give you an example. We had 28 people in our Staining Department. I thought this was too many and wanted to reduce it. By paying a few cents extra (as an incentive) for each basket stained, we ended up with nine employees doing more than the 28 had. That's motivation.

On another level, keeping the grounds and buildings clean at all times develops pride within the employees and provides a level of motivation.

Talking about the future of *their* company is very important. That is one of the elements that keeps us going. The *future* – get excited about it. Talk about it with them. Create that excitement and start organizing it to happen.

THE 12TH PRINCIPLE, J.A.R. —
JUDGMENT – ATTITUDE – RELATIONSHIPS

> "Your **JUDGMENT** and
>
> your **ATTITUDE** are directly
>
> related to your **RELATIONSHIPS**."

A good relationship can help you to overcome many shortcomings. But you must be honest with yourself first. Ask your people what they like or don't like about you. They know.

We've started a practice that has created a lot of enthusiasm, controversy and management improvement, all at the same time. We ask our *employees* to rate our *managers*. We created an evaluation form for our employees to evaluate their supervisors from time to time. This gives our supervisors a clear picture of their weaknesses and strengths.

Who knows the supervisor better than the employee? So, for example, if a manager consistently receives an overall and/or individual lower score, we're able to identify it, point it out, educate and encourage. This has not only raised employee morale, but has also strengthened relationships and sharpened managers' attitudes.

I believe that Longaberger is only as good as our employees feel. That's why I've asked the employees to evaluate their supervisors. I want to know if employees trust them, if they're available and spending time on the floor, if they're positive and set a good example. These answers tell us how well a manager is doing and it usually correlates with high or low production in that area.

Judgments depend on healthy attitudes. You can't achieve or manage without a good attitude. Attitudes are frequently determined by the quality of your relationships.

THE 13TH PRINCIPLE, E.A.R. —
ENERGY – APPEARANCE – REST

"Your **ENERGY** and

    your **APPEARANCE** are directly

        related to your **REST**."

The word Rest is by far the least thought about word by employers. We play harder than we work. Why? Because it is fun. Why not make work fun?

How do you get excited about work? First, get a good night's sleep. Encourage your employees to follow that example and to go to work thinking "If this company were mine, I would devote 25% of the day toward having fun." If they have fun they will produce. More employees will stay longer and maintain better health. The company will make it up in less benefit pay out.

I try to stop work every day at five. I think almost everyone could if they really worked during the day. Unfortunately, too many people only half-work during the day and feel like real martyrs when they stay until seven.

I think it's important to use your time off to really relax. For example, this weekend, I drove around town and then drove out to the Manufacturing Campus, sat on the bank of the lake and watched the leaves fall.

Every Wednesday and Saturday, I go to a little eating establishment. I found that things come to you while you're resting. Now whenever I come in, they give me a napkin and a pencil.

Too many people are coming into the workforce everyday dead-tired. It's not fair to you, your family, your company. You must find a way to get your rest. Nobody else can do this. If you can't manage that, how will you manage *anything?* It's up to you. I find that I am much more productive the next day when I go home and go to bed. You must start with rest.

THE 14TH PRINCIPLE, H.E.O. —
HEALTH – EXPERIENCE – OPPORTUNITY

"If you maintain your **HEALTH**,

understand the need for **EXPERIENCE**,

only then will you see **OPPORTUNITY**."

Every man and woman at age forty needs to have a stress test every two years. At age fifty, every year. You're a damn fool if you don't. If *you* don't take care of your health, who will?

One of the most exciting words I know is OPPORTUNITY!! It's there for everybody. Take myself, two years in the first grade, three years in the fifth grade, stuttered, epilepsy, poor economic background, twelve kids in the family, high school completed at twenty years of age. **The single most important thing I did and still do today is to *find a better way to do it.*** It's that simple. Some people think, if it is not hard to do, it can't be done.

Opportunity is everywhere. Open your eyes! But you say, "I don't have any money." You don't need any to get started.

The little towns around this great country of ours can be your gold mine as Dresden, Ohio was to The Longaberger Company.

We started with $135 – a small restaurant with six stools, two booths and two tables. I took $135 to buy breakfast supplies, took the money from breakfast sales and bought supplies for lunch and took the lunch money and bought supplies for dinner. We bought old buildings with a land contract.

We have come from $50,000 in sales in 1974, to hundreds of millions today. We used the restaurant to get into the grocery business, the restaurant and grocery store to get into a basket business. You can do it – it's no big deal. If you use these Principles, it can be done.

THE 15TH PRINCIPLE, S.F.F. —
STRONG – FIRM – FAIR

"Everybody will be watching

and measuring you, to see

how **STRONG**, **FIRM** and **FAIR** you are."

Strong – You cannot be mild or weak. You must have a great resource of talent. You cannot be easily upset. You must be able to endure stress, pain or vigorous growth. An unshakable dependability, high moral value, determination of spirit.

Firm – At times, you must be immovable, secure and steadfast.

Fair – You must be marked by impartiality and honesty.

You must always have that clear picture in mind. If the water gets muddy, wait until it clears before you remove anything.

You must take a stand and you must explain why at times. With this Principle, you must use the 2nd Principle, Listen to People, the 3rd Principle, Trust People and/or the 7th Principle, Market and Merchandise Yourself.

Everybody will be watching and measuring you, to see how strong, firm and fair you are. If you prove to have these qualities, you are certainly a person to do business with.

THE 16TH PRINCIPLE, L.O.B. —
LOOK – ON – BANK

"You must always be

LOOKing <u>**ON**</u> the <u>**BANK**</u>

for help and assurance

no matter who you are."

Business is like swimming. Don't go in, unless you Look On the Bank for someone to save you. In managing people, this translates that if you have a situation that you *think* you can handle, but feel some doubt, it's time to get some upper management advice.

Everybody needs somebody to talk to or a place to go to sometimes to think. From time to time, I must go away for three to four days. I find different people to talk with about difficult problems. I find different places also to work on difficult problems. Looking for help and assurance is an ongoing process.

THE 17TH PRINCIPLE, P.P.F. —
PAST – PRESENT – FUTURE

"The **PAST**

    is the **PRESENT**:

        the Present is the **FUTURE**."

The word Future goes hand in hand with the word *opportunity*. We can never forget where we came from and how this great country got where it is today.

Your past is the experience and building blocks of the present. You must figure out what you need from your past and direct the present to the future.

Take all 17 Longaberger Management Principles, combine all my thoughts about them and the 18th one will always be the driving force behind your success. It will always be the force behind *our* success.

THE 18TH PRINCIPLE, L.T.D. —
LOOK – THINK – DO

"**LOOK** at everything,

    THINK about everything,

        then **DO** something about it."

Look – To exercise the power of vision, to direct one's attention upon the future.

Think – To form a mental picture, to have an opinion, to have as an expectation.

Do – To carry out.

The other 17 Principles of Management boil down to the 18th one. L.T.D. Look and think about your life, your experience, your talent. Look hard at what you would like to do and plan it in phases.

Then you must act. Carry out your plan. Move. Work hard. Be disciplined and focused.

If you study all of the Principles closely, you will see how they relate to one another. It is perfectly alright to understand them differently from someone else. They mean different things to different people.

Having now had the opportunity to share these Principles with groups of all sizes and ages, I think the Principles come down to three little words - *Listen*, *Trust* and *Relationships*.

When you truly listen, you gain trust. When you have trust, you create a relationship. Relationships are critical in all aspects of life - especially business. Without these three words, you can't build anything.

CONSULTANTS –
THE LONGABERGER CONNECTION

"People give me the credit for Longaberger, but it's the Consultants who have made Longaberger great. It may be the Longaberger story, but the Consultants *sell* the story." – Dave Longaberger

When Charleen Cuckovich first saw a shelf of dusty baskets in that small Amish Country Ohio shop, a new chapter was written in the Longaberger story. Charleen points out that it's important to remember the baskets were dusty. That means sales weren't too brisk.

Dave was not satisfied with this sales strategy either. So when Charleen presented the idea of a basket show in someone's home, things began to happen. "As soon as she said it, I knew this was it. This was how The Longaberger Company would grow," Dave said.

"We both held parties and the response was better than even *I* had hoped for. We told them about the history of the baskets and my family and the more we told them, the more they wanted to know."

And so Charleen Cuckovich held her first show in November 1977. "I had it in my home and a week later I had another show in a friend's home. The people loved the baskets and I was getting several bookings from each show. I used the history of the Longaberger family. I showed the baskets. I told about the weavers in Dresden, a little town where many of the houses on the main drive are white and the pretty little porches have flowers.

"I admit I colored it up quite a bit too," Charleen laughed. "I remember the first time Dave came up to do a show with me. After he got to my house, we had to drive another 15 minutes through a snow storm.

"I was really excited and he was too. He said he was looking forward to hearing what I was telling these people. There were 15 or 20 ladies there that night and Dave pulled up a chair and sat right behind me. Well, I told the Longaberger story and uses for the baskets. Then I answered questions and took orders.

"One of the stories that I was particularly proud of was about this one little basket the Longaberger children had used to run down to the hen house and gather up the eggs every morning. The women loved it! Dave was beside himself, because the ladies were praising his baskets and he was joking and loving it. I still remember we got $700 and six bookings that night.

"When we got in the car, I was anxious for him to tell me that I did good, but he wasn't saying anything. He was just leaning forward with his legs crossed. Boy, was he thinking! I couldn't tell if he was happy or sad. Then, he turned and said, 'You know, Charleen, we never had chickens.' I laughed, 'Really? I just assumed the Longaberger's had chickens.' 'Nope. We never had chickens.' And then he laughed."

A LONGABERGER HOME SHOW

From that beginning, it became clear to Dave that the home shows were the way to sell his baskets.

A Consultant still markets Longaberger Baskets and much more. That's the only way anyone can buy a basket. (With the exception of the Dresden Tour Basket, you can't buy one in a store.) You have to go to a Longaberger show held in someone's home. The Consultant's role is critical to the growth and well-being of the company. Without the Consultants, there are no orders to be filled. With no orders, neither baskets nor pottery need to be made. Of course the Consultants are equally dependent on the manufacturing employees.

"Since that snowy night, the enthusiasm for Longaberger Baskets has continued to increase," Dave said. "Our products are offered across the country through tens of thousands of Consultants. Their dedication and hard work, combined with the outstanding support of our home office staff, has made The Longaberger Company a success. Our success is directly related to the success of our Consultants."

The sales field numbers have increased from just one in 1973, to more than 20,000 in 1994.

"We want to have many more Consultants than we do now," said Tami, "but we want it to be controlled growth so that we can give them the proper training and service they'll require."

Industry experts say it's unusual that most Longaberger Consultants have not previously sold for other direct sales companies. Many had never been to a home party before coming to a Longaberger show. So although there's little experience or training in the Consultants' background, there's also little bias or controversial sales methods.

The Consultants we spoke to were first attracted to the company out of a love for Longaberger Baskets. Not only do they have them throughout their home, but they truly enjoy showing them to others. In other words, they still love the baskets.

Even the top Sales Associates in personal sales and recruiting receive a specially designed basket among other awards at the Bee.

As we've seen several times already, the Longaberger show allows the Consultant to create an atmosphere of warmth, a step back in time, old fashioned American quality and a warm feeling for the Longaberger family. As Jan Brunstetter, an Ohio Consultant said, "You're not just telling the story of how a quality basket is made. You're also establishing the emotion that goes along with the basket."

Consumers don't receive a message like that when they pick up a product from a shelf in a store. It may also be a product that competes with several other similar products on the same shelf. The home show is a unique sales environment.

Tami analyzed, "From a strictly business standpoint, the home show is our best marketing tool. Why should we go any other route? Why would we hassle with department stores, buying shelf space and worrying about where the next order is going to come from? I am convinced that we sell more products today through our Consultants than we ever would through those retail stores who would also insist upon profit margins that would make a hand-made basket nearly impossible to sell.

"I read recently that consumers have gone from *shop till you drop* in the '80s to *drop shopping* in the '90s. Customers want consistent value, convenience, personalized service and an enjoyable shopping experience. Longaberger provides all of this."

> AS WE'VE SEEN SEVERAL TIMES ALREADY, THE LONGABERGER SHOW ALLOWS THE CONSULTANT TO CREATE AN ATMOSPHERE OF WARMTH, A STEP BACK IN TIME, OLD FASHIONED AMERICAN QUALITY AND A WARM FEELING FOR THE LONGABERGER FAMILY.

"Women have made our company what it is today," Dave observed. "Women buy the products. They see its value and appreciate our story.

"And now the company is being led by two women, my two daughters. That's very exciting! Without these two women, Longaberger's future would not be nearly as successful!"

A SALES CAREER WITH LONGABERGER

Family, career and more . . . You *can* have it all!

Women today have so many choices to make. Family or career? Part-time or full-time? Creative or practical? Traditional or progressive? Work or leisure? Fun or profit?

The ideal working situation has a fine balance of all of these ingredients. And for thousands of women, Longaberger is the ideal solution. A Longaberger Sales Associate lives the life she wants to lead, according to her priorities.

"Longaberger affords you the opportunity to have it all," Tami says. "Personal development, improved self esteem, a flexible schedule, and an overall better quality of life for your family can be achieved with Longaberger. And there's no 'glass ceiling.' If you're dedicated and work hard, Longaberger can take you as far as you want to go. You can change your life for the better."

It's no wonder more than one Longaberger Sales Associate has been heard to say, "If it's too good to be true, it must be Longaberger!"

Betty Palm, Vice President of Sales and Marketing, adds, "Consultants should also possess discipline and perseverance. You cannot get discouraged. You have to stay with it. But Longaberger Consultants are fortunate because our products are so unique. Our sales force loves the products and they pass that enthusiasm and appreciation on to Longaberger customers."

National Sales Director Anita Rector agrees. "Many of our Consultants have never sold any other direct sales products. Many had never been to a direct sales party of any kind. They are impressed immediately by the beauty of the baskets and pottery. The more they learn about the Longaberger history and about Dave, Tami and Rachel, the more impressed they become. We don't hard-sell anyone to become a Consultant. The baskets really sell themselves." This helps explain why Longaberger enjoys one of the lowest turnover rates in the industry.

The Consultants are a diverse group. Several professions are represented, including teachers, professors, nurses, homemakers, weavers, farmers and full-time Consultants. Although many live somewhat close to Dresden, thousands live throughout the United States.

Roxanne Krebs, a Regional Advisor and former school teacher from Omaha, Nebraska, remembers her early days with Longaberger. "I had to change my attitude from education to sales. I had a problem with having a college degree and selling baskets. Once I was able to reconcile that issue, my sales took off and within a year I became a Branch Advisor and moved into a full-time career."

Roxanne sees opportunities with Longaberger as exciting for several reasons. "One is simply the fact that with so many women working, it provides them with an opportunity to do their shopping without going to the malls. They can come into a home, relax and have a cup of coffee with their friends and yet be presented with quality products that they can purchase conveniently. Second, catalog shopping is growing on a national basis. However, with us, you also have the chance to view the product, touch it, feel it and hear somebody talk about it. Of course, once they're familiar with the product, they can just call me over the phone and tell me what they want. They haven't had to leave their home and the product will be shipped directly to them.

"I still point out that anyone beginning with Longaberger now is very much on the ground floor, especially here in Nebraska!"

"Many have given up professional jobs for a few years to raise children and stumble onto The Longaberger Company and find it is something they can do for a few years while they raise their children," Sales Director Joan Henning said. "Then many decide they like it better than their previous professions and stay with us."

"A career selling Longaberger products is more appealing than ever," Betty Palm said. "In an era of corporate down sizing, it makes sense to have more control over your future. Being a Longaberger Consultant allows you to structure your career around your family - not the other way around. A Consultant's business offers flexibility, control and is home-based."

Through recruiting others, Consultants not only earn more, but also move into management positions such as Branch Advisor, Regional Advisor or Sales Director.

"Consultants tell me how much Longaberger has done for their lives," Tami said. "I hear, 'I used to be insecure but now I'm standing in front of people holding shows. I feel needed and important!' "

Indeed, the Consultants are told often they're important. They're applauded at meetings. They're recognized at the annual Bees. They're told "good job" by peers. They get positive feedback from their customers. It builds self-confidence in many Consultants who never had it before.

"Being with The Longaberger Company really brought me out of myself," agreed Mary Pilchak, Regional Advisor from Findlay, Ohio. Mary was a first grade teacher when she happened to see the "World's Largest Basket" at the Ohio State Fair. She started as a part-time Consultant. Mary soon went to work for Longaberger full time "because my business just grew and grew."

Carol Robinson, a Branch Advisor from Rushsylvania, Ohio, was also at the Ohio State Fair that year. "While watching the sheep show, I became bored and began walking when I saw the biggest basket I'd ever seen! I went through it several times. I'd just quit a good job so I wasn't thinking of anything but how fascinating I found all of these baskets.

I heard them say they needed someone with experience in meeting people in my area. I found myself saying I could do that. I was asked if I'd like to book a show. Well, I'd not been to a home show in about ten years. I didn't like them. But I heard myself say, 'No, I think I'd like to sell them!' Then I thought, 'Who said that?'

"I went back to my husband at the sheep show and told him I had a job. He thought I had really lost it and was going to sell pop or something at the fairgrounds! He was just as impressed as I was though. We told our daughter and she drove all the way to Columbus to see for herself and she was sold.

"As I look back on my career, our basket business has been like the time I was caught in a terrible storm on the way home from my first Bee. The storms of life have rolled over us with a fervor at times, but we always spring back, holding a basket! When things have gone sour in my personal life, I used the basket business as a refuge to save my sanity. In good times, we fill a basket and celebrate.

"My daughter, Cindy, was the first daughter to branch (become a Branch Advisor) from her mother in the history of our company.

"Whenever someone asks why I have stayed through all our crises, the only thing I can say is that it would never occur to me to leave a family member in the lurch when they needed me. And why would I want to leave when things are good?!

"I love bringing in a new Consultant and seeing her go on and on about the friendliness of everyone involved, how they can walk up and speak to the family or staff, how they feel like family and how much potential there is for them here. I hope I never cease to be surprised at their pleasure with our company."

When Vicki Sugar, Sales Director, moved to Granville, Ohio, in 1979, the only person she knew invited her to a basket show. Vicki expected wicker and upon seeing the wood, initially thought they all looked the same. "But after the Consultant started telling the history of the baskets, I wanted to buy every one of them!" she explained.

Vicki remembered, "I had been a learning disabilities teacher for three years with a child on the way. I decided to quit teaching and have been with Longaberger ever since."

Vicki has over 200 Consultants across the nation. "Selling the baskets and pottery has given me some of my closest friends," she reflected. "And, I found I had the opportunity to earn what a doctor earns, by enjoying myself and helping others discover Longaberger products."

Paula Vandegriff, Sales Director, had moved to Virginia and was looking for a way to supplement her family's income. She came across Longaberger Baskets in 1979. "I was impressed with the quality of the baskets and thought they would sell well here. Their quality and family tradition really sold them."

Elaine Swaintek is a Regional Advisor from Alburtis, Pennsylvania. Her business grew so much that she teaches art only part-time now. "My association with The Longaberger Company has been extremely successful for me financially and personally. It's given me the privilege to stay home and raise my children and have a successful career."

Debbie Baber from Roanake, Virginia, became a Consultant in 1981 because she wanted to work full time but still stay home with her children. "I made the decision that my niche at Longaberger was in management. I prioritized each day. I'd look at my list of things to do and ask myself, 'What on this list will get me to Sales Director?' and I'd do that thing first." Eleven years later, she became a Sales Director.

"I started working with my recruits. I helped them realize their management potential and helped them build Branches - and then build Branches into Regions."

Debbie has rarely led in sales, yet her focus on leadership enabled her to become a Sales Director.

"Although I take a professional approach to my career with Longaberger, my family's needs still come first. I don't want to miss soccer games or swim meets. That's why I've never chosen to be top in sales."

Debbie recalls life-threatening complications when she was pregnant with her third child causing her to be hospitalized for more than two months. "My paycheck never stopped, thanks to my group members for keeping the sales going. My sister is in real estate and we might make the same income, but if she were sick for three months, never would her paycheck continue like mine did."

Debbie says the rewards of leadership keep her motivated and inspired. "It is just the neatest thing to watch a Consultant grow. She comes into this business with a low self-esteem and finally someone says to her, 'Hey, you've done a great job!' The next time you see her maybe she has her hair fixed up or a new outfit, maybe she's won a few awards. Then one day she walks up on stage at the Bee and I think, 'Wow, I helped her.' That is so rewarding!"

Debbie operates her Directorship from her mountain-top home. "I have the privilege to be here and watch my baby grow and still hold a top management position in the Longaberger sales field. I believe I have the best of both worlds."

Regional Advisor Barb Scholten said, "I tell potential or new Consultants that they can be truly anything they want to be. You don't have to lead in sales. You don't have to let it run your life. There are single moms supporting their families. I know advisors who have put their children through medical school. You can earn an extra $300 a month or make it a full time career. I want to make it very clear to them that they can make it what they want it to be, and I'll be there right behind them!"

A Tour Through Dresden

Dresden, population 1,500, has changed dramatically in the last few years. Let's take a tour. As we drive into Dresden, you'll notice a very unique welcome sign. The bottom part of the sign is actually made out of the same maple strips the baskets are created with.

Let's begin at the northern part of town. But before we turn off the highway, see the house Dave built at the top of the hill? It's pretty hard to miss. That's where he camped out as a boy – on "Machine Gun Hill." (This seven-level structure is now used for corporate meetings and entertaining the top Sales Consultants during the Bee.)

Our first stop is the **Corporate Office,** formerly **Plant One.** It's really seen a change! It has been totally renovated from housing the weavers, who have moved to the Manufacturing Campus. It houses the executive and administrative offices. Office space fills up the old weaving floor. This building has seen a lot of changes since the day that Dave looked through the window and saw trees growing through the ceiling.

We leave the Corporate Office and turn onto Main Street, where you'll get your first glimpse of this quaint, storybook village. New sidewalks, new curbs, new grass and trees between the sidewalk and street and even new street baskets filled with colorful flowers and plants.

The striking building on the left with flower boxes under each window is **The Longaberger Restaurant.** First owned by Dave, you'll recall, in the 1960s, it's a 160-seat home cooking facility. Talk about Longaberger decor – wait until you see this place. Baskets on the walls, baskets on the shelves, and even your food is served in Longaberger Pottery and Baskets. This is a real favorite for the residents and hungry visitors.

THE LONGABERGER RESTAURANT

From here, we'll walk. That's one of the nice things about Dresden. It's a good place to walk. It provides great small town America scenery and atmosphere and if you're not in too big a hurry, you can walk about anywhere you want to go. As we walk, you'll notice a variety of attractive shops and homes. And by the time I've told you this, we have come to **Popeye's.**

POPEYE'S

This is the focal point of the village, in my opinion. It's a '50s style place, complete with '50s music, juke boxes at every booth, black and white tile floor, stamped tin ceiling, neon lights, waitresses in '50s style clothes. It's flat tops, Mickey Mantle, pony tails, Elvis Presley, Marilyn Monroe *and* a fun place to eat. You'll also like their Popeye's T-Shirts with the Juke Box logo.

Now that you're as full as a Longaberger Basket purse, let's go across the street and check out **The Longaberger Museum**.

This is where you can learn about the Dresden Shuttle which not only takes you around Dresden, but also takes you to and from the Manufacturing Campus. Let's take a minute to look through a few pages of the guest register. You may be surprised at how many states are represented. The tour through the museum begins in the video theater. What better place to see a short film about the past, present and future of The Longaberger Company than in the middle of Dresden, in The Longaberger Museum? After the video, the doors at the back of the

THE LONGABERGER MUSEUM

theater are opened to reveal several exhibits which show the birth and growth of the company. The museum also contains many of J.W. Longaberger's original baskets, displayed in a 1930s setting.

There is also a weaver actually weaving baskets, letting you see first hand the skill and artistry involved in this age-old craft. There are many interesting exhibits, so take your time. The museum opened on August 4, 1990. It coincided with the Bee. One day of the Bee is proclaimed "Dresden Day," so thousands of Longaberger Consultants annually come to town to see what we're presently touring.

Upon leaving the museum, you'll see a giant basket. We'll walk across the street to the pretty little park and read the sign, **"The World's Largest Basket** – Guiness Book." It's made with the same maple wood from which all other Longaberger Baskets are made – but with larger strips. Just for the record, it's 23 feet high (from the ground to the handles), 19 feet wide and 48 feet long. It was handwoven from ten hardwood maple trees. Try to work that into a conversation soon.

Just down the street are the **Main Street Shops**. **The Village Gift Shop**, is where you'll find collectible teddy bears and Yankee candles. **The Breakfast Shop and More** features fresh cinnamon rolls, French toast and a full menu of traditional breakfast foods, as well as light luncheon fare. **The Dresden Colony House** offers a beautiful assortment of home accessories, framed prints, Christmas collectibles and hand-painted ceramic basket tie-ons. The **Village Etc. Shop** is filled with Longaberger memorabilia to take home.

Across the street is the Dresden IGA, Dave's old grocery store. Also, on Main Street, is what was originally The Grand Hotel. On the first floor, you'll find men's and women's apparel. On the second floor, you'll discover an art and furniture gallery.

Down the street we go to **Jayhawks Dairy Bar,** which features high school memorabilia and an open-air eating spot with live entertainment.

A couple of streets down, on Chestnut, between Seventh and Eighth Streets, is **Longaberger University**, a training facility for Longaberger's employees and sales force. "This will be, of all places, in my old grade school building, in the middle of Dresden. If my fifth grade teacher were still alive, she'd go into cardiac arrest. If someone had walked into that classroom one of the three years I occupied it, and said, 'In a few decades, one of you will buy this building and turn it into a university,' not one person would have guessed it would have been me.

"When we walked around in the building not long ago, I walked up to my old fifth grade room and looked around. When we turned to walk out of the room, I told the others that there was some force that was pulling me back into it.

THE WORLD'S LARGEST BASKET

"When I retire, I plan to put my office in that old fifth grade classroom."

Walking back to Main Street, we arrive at **The Station House**, another remodeled structure in town, used for meetings and banquets.

A few steps away, **The Dresden Depot**, restored by Longaberger, reflects the feel of a time gone by. These days, the Depot hosts special holiday events for children and provides a nice resting spot anytime of the year. If you're lucky, the train will arrive while you're there.

THE DRESDEN DEPOT

A short distance away is **The Senior Citizens Center.** It's a very popular and active place. It provides a convenient meeting place for the village's seniors, and a hot lunch is served each weekday.

In this area is **Kenny Wolford Community Park**, named in honor of longtime Dresden Police and Fire Chief, Kenny Wolford. The park was created by Longaberger for the youth of Dresden. It's impressive. It includes five lighted baseball fields, a football field, soccer field, basketball courts and volleyball courts, a picnic area and continues to expand.

The park also includes **The Fitness Center**. There's no need to skip your exercise routine while visiting Dresden. You'll find an indoor basketball court, aerobics classes, Nautilus, free weights, racquetball, wallyball and, of course, showers and lockers.

KENNY WOLFORD COMMUNITY PARK

Located within the park is **The Swimming Center**. Swim in the world's largest stainless steel pool which accommodates up to 800 people. The center also offers an unusually large landscaped patio for sunbathing and picnicking. The building offers a community room, fully equipped locker rooms and a restaurant, **The Hangout**. The Swimming Center is enhanced by beautiful, decorative brick work. "I see it as a one-time expense," Dave explains. "This building should be around for Dresden and our visitors to enjoy for over a century. I think it makes sense to build it with style and beauty."

THE SWIMMING CENTER

A PARK ON DRESDEN'S MAIN STREET.

The last stop on Main Street is **Longaberger Construction and WoodCrafts**, formerly **Plant Three.**

But we have one more stop to make for the tour's grand finale – **the Manufacturing Campus**. Building A is 250,000 square feet. Building B is 850,000 square feet. The Manufacturing Campus is beautifully landscaped with cascading water over rocks in one of the two ponds. The roads are lined with hundreds of maple trees, symbolic of the maple wood used in Longaberger baskets. The campus also includes the Employee Development Center, Landscaping and Nursery facilities, a Handle building, Manufacturing, Security and Safety building and Inventory buildings.

As a part of the tour, you'll ascend the stairs to an observation walkway to witness hundreds of Longaberger manufacturing employees in action. It's an impressive sight. You'll see L-TV, Longaberger Television, in action, on the hundred-plus televisions mounted above the manufacturing floor. You'll also want to visit the **Just For Fun** shop located on the observation level.

This completes the tour, but rest assured that on your next visit to Dresden, there will be more to see and do!

TOURISTS CAN WATCH EVERY STAGE OF THE BASKET MAKING PROCESS.

THE CAPTAIN'S HOUSE, BEFORE RENOVATION. BUILT IN THE 1800S, IT'S ONE BLOCK OFF MAIN STREET.

THE CAPTAIN'S HOUSE, AFTER. THE LONGABERGER COMPANY ACQUIRED THE HISTORIC HOUSE IN THE 1980S FOR FUTURE EXPANSION.

THE BEE
THE WORLD'S LARGEST BASKET SHOW

The highlight of each year takes place at the Bee. Thousands of Consultants descend on Columbus, Ohio, mid-summer. They renew acquaintances, make new ones, share ideas and soak up the experience.

One of the benefits of the Bee is for Consultants to be recognized for their achievements. Consultants are recognized, on stage, in front of thousands of their peers, in such categories as sales, recruiting and management. The awards are presented by Sales Directors, company executives and members of the Longaberger family.

On Dresden Day, Consultants visit Dresden, touring, eating and shopping. With thousands of Longaberger Consultants visiting at the same time, Dresden takes on a festive atmosphere.

They visit the weavers and employees at the plants in Dresden and Hartville. They see the lathe create veneer sheets and watch the guillotine cut the splints. They see the splints dipped into the dyes. They watch the weavers make baskets. But there's more. They can even make their own baskets! With the assistance of the weavers, the Consultants weave, tack and sign their baskets. And then keep them forever.

The Bee also provides opportunities to say "thank you," as family members should. It's not unusual to overhear a Consultant run up to a shipping department employee, for example, and say, "My, what a wonderful job you do in packing. I haven't had a basket damaged yet." Not only do employees and Consultants establish friendships at the Bee, but they also nourish them through letters and Holiday cards.

Then there are picnics, a recognition lunch at Dave's former home, games, visits with Tami, Rachel, and other Longaberger family members.

The Bee is a shot in the arm to Consultants. The sales field has grown so large that, in 1993, it began to require two Bees. Alice Hanley, a Branch Advisor from Clear Lake, Iowa, says, "I go to all the Bees. It helps me see the big picture and the potential of a Longaberger career."

In some ways, the Bee is like a giant basket show. It's a celebration of the Longaberger products. It's several thousand people who are committed to keeping the quality alive.

The Bee is important because it serves as a family reunion. It serves as a kick-off. And it serves as a way of saying "thank you for a great job!"

GRANDMA BONNIE!

PRESENT...CONCLUDING THOUGHTS

The manufacturing, the marketing, the people, the shows, the plants, the projects . . . the present has become big business for The Longaberger Company. And yet, the attitude seems to be "You ain't seen nothin' yet!"

Maybe that's why they've grown, because they've always had that attitude and believed it. No one thought a man could run a four-minute mile until Roger Bannister did it. No one thought heavier-than-air objects could provide transportation until Frank and Orville Wright did it. No one thought Jack Nicklaus could win the Masters again at an advanced age. Or that 5'7" Spudd Webb could win the NBA dunk contest. Or that Ronald Reagan could be elected President in his 70s. Or that NASA could put a man on the moon.

But they did, because they believed they could. And what if they couldn't reach their ultimate goal? Aren't they still successful by being that much closer to their goal than they were? Dave Longaberger thinks so.

THE OLD BASKET SHOP

I think a very clear message comes from the Longaberger Story: *Don't be afraid to try*. You have to consider the risks involved (Look), contemplate your strategy (Think) and then begin (Do). As the Chinese saying goes, "A journey of 1,000 miles begins with the first step." Or as an American saying goes, "Footprints in the sands of time were never made while sitting down." You've got to start.

I've been impressed that Dave totally committed himself to his goal. It was essential to have that type of zeal to overcome the many obstacles. Therefore, the other message is: *Be ready to do what it takes*. It will take more than you thought.

Perhaps there's even a third message: *Enjoy it*. It may be stressful and the hours may be long, but if you don't enjoy the climb, it's not worth the view.

I'm not sure it's possible to do justice to the current activities at Longaberger in a book. It varies with the people you meet and the season you're there. Perhaps the specific day-to-day activities aren't as important as the mood of the employees and Consultants. Once you've seen that, it's easy to understand how the pride in the past and the hope of the future come together today.

When Tami Longaberger stood up at a Bee, she said, "Welcome to the Bee and welcome to our family reunion!" Applause interrupted her, erupting from every corner of the Columbus Convention Center. Consultants stood in unison and cheered because Tami acknowledged what they already realized. "We're family."

VISION FOR TOMORROW AWARD

In 1990, Dave Longaberger received the first *Vision for Tomorrow* Award at the annual convention of the Direct Selling Association (DSA) in Scottsdale, Arizona.

The DSA convention brought together more than 600 chief executives of America's largest direct selling companies, including Home Interiors and Gifts, Tupperware, Avon and Mary Kay.

RACHEL, DAVE AND TAMI IN DAVE'S OFFICE.

The award was presented to a company which substantially improved the quality of life for its community. Presented for outstanding community service, the *Vision for Tomorrow* Award recognized Longaberger for its revitalization of Dresden.

Let me tell you a secret. Dave wasn't even going to the convention. Tami received a call before the convention, informing her of the committee's decision. She wanted the award to be a surprise, so she concocted a reason for Dave to go and he agreed.

"It turned out to be one of the biggest surprises of my life," Dave recalled. "As they were describing the award, I leaned over to Tami and said, 'In two or three years we could be a candidate for that.' She just nodded."

When they announced that the winner was Dave Longaberger, he was completely surprised. He sat there, stunned, while he received a standing ovation.

When he walked up front to receive the award, he was informed a video had been quickly produced in preparation for that evening, to share Dresden with the other companies.

THE 12 LONGABERGER CHILDREN WITH GRANDMA BONNIE.

"As I watched our tiny village on that screen and realized that all of these other major companies were looking at our efforts in Dresden, my eyes watered up and I was filled with a great sense of pride," Dave recalled.

"This honor belongs to all our employees and everyone involved in our national sales program," Dave said as he accepted the award. "They made it possible through hard work and dedication. I'm indebted to them and to the Direct Selling Association which has done so much over the years to help our business grow and mature."

In thinking about the award later, Dave reflected, "I firmly believe that companies should put money back into their communities. It makes me so mad that corporations want tax breaks. Let politicians do what they were paid to do and not cater to corporations who say, 'We're not going to move into this area unless we get a 15-year deal.'

"One of the accomplishments that I'm proudest of is that we've never asked for a tax abatement. I say that it's up to companies to supply money for parks to increase the quality of life for their communities.

"I believe very strongly in giving back to your community and your employees. If you don't, you aren't much of a person. If you don't have gratitude, you've overlooked a big part of life. It will eventually come back to get you personally and professionally."

As Assistant Vice President of Guest Services Ron Buchenroth put it, "What Dave predicted is coming true. People are coming to Dresden because of word of mouth. The customer now not only buys our products, but also falls in love with our company."

Dave explains, "Our company's Mission Statement is to *stimulate a better quality of life*. We provide that for Dresden by helping to provide a good work base, good schools, good recreational facilities, good community organizations, good roads, housing, restaurants and shops."

Longaberger has also been honored with the Department of Interior's Take Pride in America Award in 1991; the 1992 *Inc.* Magazine's Most Socially Responsible Entrepreneur; and the 1993 ChildHelp Award for "helping children and families succeed."

THE FUTURE

THE "HUMAN WOVEN L."
MORE THAN 1,000 LONGABERGER EMPLOYEES
GATHERED AT THE MANUFACTURING CAMPUS
TO CREATE THE LONGABERGER LOGO.

LONGABERGER — MORE TO COME...

Dave Longaberger talks about the future. A lot. If you happen to be with him very long, you'll notice it too.

Dave constantly sees future trends in business. He sees them because of his experiences in the past. For example, he sees that for American businesses to compete, they're going to have to be more customer and employee oriented. Corporate leaders will also have to come out of their boardrooms and reserved parking spaces and into the everyday environment of their employees. They'll need the trust of their employees to succeed. To get that trust, they must prove their commitment to the employees and the customers.

"I seriously believe you, the reader, would make a better leader than 75% of the leaders in corporations today," Dave said. "A lot of them were put there because of *who* they knew, not *what* they knew.

"A few years ago, I thought it best to remove myself as Chief Executive Officer. I felt that I was not the best person to run the company. After all, I didn't have a college degree and I had made a few mistakes. I was convinced that someone with more education and intelligence could be much more effective than I was.

"So that's what I did. I replaced myself with someone else. This was by far the most critical time in my life, because I had given up on me. I thought the company would be better off without me.

"I'll never forget that day. Driving home after turning it over to the new executive, I felt very low, about the same as when I sold the restaurant. I bought into the idea that my management practices were wrong and needed to be changed.

"Only then did I hear my employees and Consultants call me foolish. Not for making mistakes, but for not giving myself credit.

"I began to take inventory of myself. I felt like I had strong people skills. I nurtured a company with no money and a car full of baskets into a multi-million dollar company. I recognized opportunities. I was able to motivate, negotiate and sell. I was honest and straightforward in my dealings with employees and customers. I had a good sense of humor. I enjoyed being with people. I enjoyed work. I also knew that I had a lot of common sense.

"I began to see that although I certainly had weaknesses, I also had a great many strengths. And you do too! Sometimes you just have to step away from a situation before you recognize them.

"Like a fool, I believed that everything I'd done in the past was wrong and anything I'd done right was just luck. But then I woke up and came back. If I hadn't, I believe much harm would have been done, simply because I didn't give myself the credit I deserved.

"This is a lesson for you. Don't let someone tell you that you don't know anything. If you make a mistake, admit it, but don't give up on yourself. Learn from the mistakes. I firmly believe that suffering from and surviving through my mistakes has made me stronger.

"I think this is a key to the future: You have to believe in yourself and in the ability of others. Without others, you're nothing. Whether it's good or bad, you can learn something from everyone you meet. Listen and learn from the people you meet everyday. It's free.

"Go to school on people. Simply watch their reactions. What makes them happy? What makes them sad? I think the most important sports game that's played is the universal sport of winning people's trust. People trusting you. It's very simple, but it's vital. You may think you have everything to get ahead. No trust, no future. I guess universities don't teach this people skill because it's too simple. Perhaps they believe if the idea is too simple, it shouldn't be taught."

Dave Longaberger has always looked to the future. He believes that the future provides motivation for all of us. He incorporates the future in his daily conversation. He shares his vision of the future with employees, Consultants and friends. He is always looking ahead.

I've heard him talk about some exciting and some unique (some even strange!) things he plans to do in the future. That seems to be a common trait of successful entrepreneurs – being able to envision what isn't. Spotting opportunity the way a collector spots a rare coin. Forecasting customer demands the way a meteorologist predicts rain.

THE LONGABERGER COMPANY
20 YEAR PLAN

In August 1991, Dave spent two weeks in a Pinehurst, North Carolina, condominium. He returned with *The Longaberger Company 20 Year Plan*. It represented an ambitious view of the company's growth and sales. It was based on a growth rate of 25% per year. As you will see, the future is proving brighter than Dave predicted.

The last year in Longaberger's Plan is 2010. The plan projects that the total number of Consultants will be 125,000 and total number of employees will be 31,000. As ambitious as those projections sound, remember that the actual figures are already significantly exceeding his plan. It's no wonder why Dave is excited about the future!

"Coming up with the 20 year plan was the easy part," Dave laughed. "Tami and Rachel have to make it work!"

Dresden – Preparing for the 21st Century

The Longaberger Company has created a 10 year plan for the Dresden area. The company's efforts are focused on five ingredients necessary to make a community successful.

The Five Ingredients for a Successful Community

1. **Employment** - The Longaberger Company is one of the largest employers in central Ohio. As the company has increased, new employment opportunities have been created. The company offers an array of benefits and employee care programs. By 1995, the company plans to have a day care center operating for children of employees, and a Longaberger Convenience Center, complete with a grocery, bank and laundry/dry cleaning facility. A very health-conscious company, Longaberger maintains a smoke-free environment and has declared a war on drugs.

2. **Education** - As Dave said, "If only I'd received more education, I'd be dangerous." Dave is turning his failure in education into tangible educational opportunities for the community.

When citizens voted against a proposed bond levy to add necessary classrooms to Dresden's Tri-Valley High School, The Longaberger

Company provided millions of dollars to fund the project. The result was the addition of 23 much-needed classrooms, two science labs, a multi-purpose band and choir room, and a separate vocational agricultural center.

Longaberger is also committed to other area schools. A few examples include: a grant to the Par Excellence Learning Center in Newark to develop academic achievement among underprivileged children. Longaberger provided a grant to Welsh Hills School (a private, alternative school) in Granville, Ohio, to help build a new facility. Longaberger has also awarded an endowment to a local school in Zanesville.

3. **Recreation** - Dave Longaberger feels that in order for a community to thrive, it must enjoy quality recreation. The Longaberger Company has developed several programs and facilities for the Dresden community: The Kenny Wolford Community Park, The Fitness Center, The Swimming Center and The Dresden Senior Citizens Center.

THE SENIOR CITIZENS CENTER

THE LONGABERGER COMPANY PROVIDED MILLIONS OF DOLLARS TO ADD NECESSARY CLASSROOMS TO TRI-VALLEY HIGH SCHOOL.

4. **Roads and Housing** - During the past several years, the company and community have experienced phenomenal growth. Employees travel from throughout Central and Eastern Ohio to Longaberger facilities. Tourism has also become an important industry in Dresden. With the increased number of people using roadways in the area, safety becomes a priority.

At a cost of $300,000, Longaberger added turn lanes and traffic lights to State Route 16 in front of the manufacturing campus to increase the safety of the thousands of employees and tourists. This was a very proactive move for a private company, since this cost is normally absorbed by the government. After it was complete, the company gave the property to the state.

Adequate housing facilities are also of concern. Longaberger's rapid growth has increased residential construction throughout the area. Longaberger is also assisting Zanesville's Habitat for Humanity. A crew from Longaberger Construction helped refurbish several homes for families who otherwise could not afford to become homeowners.

5. **Community Organizations** - The Longaberger Company has been recognized by local, state and national organizations for contributions made to revitalize Dresden. In addition to its concern for the Dresden area, Longaberger has also helped groups in the surrounding counties. Some of those community organizations include: a year-round residential program for the developmentally disabled in Coshocton County, construction assistance for a Salvation Army homeless shelter, the renovation of the Coshocton County YWCA for a new day care facility and assistance to area United Way agencies, to name but a few.

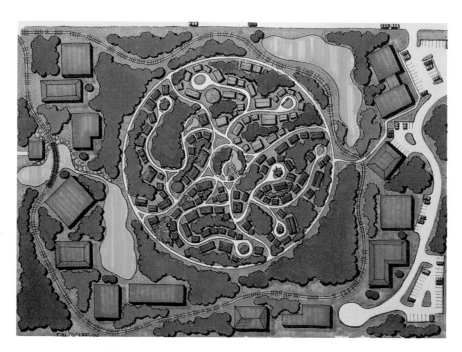

THE LONGABERGER BASKET VILLAGE

THE LONGABERGER FAMILY RESTAURANT

LONGABERGER FUTURE PLANS

Dave has a lot of plans for the future. He doesn't know if he'll put them all into effect. He doesn't even know if they'll all work. But he does have plans. For example:

Longaberger Family Restaurants. "This corporation will be franchised out, so please save your money! This will be an 11,000 square foot, two level restaurant. Good old country cooking, Grandma Bonnie's recipes, with plants and Longaberger Baskets and Pottery all over. It will tell the Longaberger story. It will look exactly like our large Market Basket with two swinging handles on it, and with the handles up, it will stand over 45 feet tall. This will work hand in hand with Longaberger marketing."

Longaberger Village. "This is my ultimate dream. To see this happen before I die. In the Northeastern United States there is not a big attraction and this is the most densely populated area of the country. Our Village will be big. All buildings within the village may take on the size and the appearance of all of our baskets. The basket buildings will contain shops, restaurants, museums and theatres. There will be no vehicles allowed in the village. It will be built in several phases.

"Outside the village will be hotels, convention centers and campgrounds."

LONGABERGER EXPERIENCES

Envisioning that the number of tourists to Dresden will continue to increase by the hundreds of thousands, Longaberger realized the need for more activities or attractions. Dave Longaberger envisions several new projects.

Longaberger Farms - Already in its first phase of development, the farm will encompass a working ranch with a recreation of an old western town and regular family-oriented entertainment programs with a Wild West flavor. "The farm is going to be big," Dave said. "Every day there will be a rodeo. So, you just happened to get there on the day of a rodeo. We'll have a huge barn for quarter horses and one for black angus cattle."

The Longaberger Golf Complex - Four major golf courses are planned: two Par Threes for beginning and intermediate players, an Advanced course and a Masters course. The property will include a tennis complex and a resort hotel. "This entire complex will be second to none," Dave advised.

The Longaberger Institute of American Business - The heartland of America - central Ohio - is an ideal place for a national conference. The Longaberger Company has purchased and is renovating the historic Soldiers and Sailors Auditorium in Newark to house the Institute. The Conference Center will be available to Longaberger and businesses nationwide to host meetings and lecture series. "People are tired of going to expensive conventions, plagued with security problems," Dave observed. "It's more productive to come to the heartland where there are family values, a more restful climate, yet with tremendous recreational opportunities."

Dresden - As you've already read, there's plenty to see and do in Dresden. The number of tourists visiting Dresden validates this point. The tourist population continues to exceed expectations. For example, in 1991, 60,000 tourists were anticipated; 75,000 came. In 1993, over 400,000 guests showed up. Over a million tourists are projected to visit in 1997. The increasing numbers made it clear that other attractions were vital to preserve Dresden's small town charm while enhancing the tourist's experience.

DAVE LONGABERGER, STC

But the list isn't over yet. Dave thinks up future projects constantly. One word of clarification. These projects will always be altered. As a matter of fact, many employees write 'Dave Longaberger, STC,' meaning 'subject to change.'

"The construction crew hates to see me coming because I always want to change something in the plans," Dave laughed.

Donna Logsdon, an employee of Dave's restaurant, grocery and basket plant, remembered, "Every time Dave sat in a booth at the restaurant and stared out the window, we said, 'Uh oh,' because something was about to change!"

I think that's an important trait to remember about Dave. Although he believes in planning for the future, he also doesn't mind altering those plans to meet existing conditions.

THE STORY CONTINUES

"I think Longaberger has the opportunity to be the best and largest Direct Sales Company in the world," Tami predicted. "We have the balance of ethics, morals and growth. There is a quite evident and growing national desire for Longaberger products and what they represent. Our challenge is not to accomplish the growth, but to manage it."

Dave believes that we all need something to look forward to and he hopes that the employees, Sales Associates and customers will look forward to the future of his ("our" Dave would say) company.

The future brings change and most of us don't like change. Dave doesn't mind it. As a matter of fact, I think he likes it. That makes him very flexible for the future and I think it's made a big difference in his ability to seize opportunity.

The fact that a lot of us want to remain the same makes us resist change until we're forced to change. It's something to think about. Change is usually not desired, but it's often for the best. Just ask Dave Longaberger.

And if you *should* ask Dave about the future, you'll probably see a twinkle in his eye and hear enthusiasm in his voice because it's a part of *The Longaberger Story* yet to be written.

EPILOGUE

It's been a real experience to go back to when I was six years old to look at the people, the places and the things that have made me who and what I am today. Through this process, I have seen my strengths and weaknesses in black and white.

Working with Steve on this book has made me stronger about my beliefs and principles. If I can tell you anything from my experiences, it's to listen to yourself first and to believe in yourself. If this book only sells a few copies, it has been invaluable to me. I've been afforded the opportunity to stop and look at who I am and who I'm going to be.

Please do this. If you don't learn anything else from my story, please do the same thing yourself. Find a place away from everyone and look at the people, places and things of your past that contribute to who you are today. Then think about where you are and who you are. Then think about where you want to be. And enjoy the process!

Dave Longaberger

For more information about Longaberger Baskets, Pottery, or other products, or for finding a Longaberger Consultant in your area write or call:

The Longaberger Company

P.O. Box 73
95 Chestnut Street
Dresden, Ohio 43821–0073
1-800-966-0374
614-754-5000

About The Author

Stephen Douglas Williford enjoys speaking to Longaberger Sales Consultants. He received the PICA Award for *The Longaberger Story,* which has sold over 200,000 copies. His latest book is *When You Really Embarrass Yourself, Nobody Ever Forgets*. Steve lives with his wife and two children in Memphis, Tennessee.